LOOPS

L∞PS

The Seven Keys to Small Business Success

**Mike Chaet, Ph.D.
and Stephen C. Lundin, Ph.D.**
with Vince Moravek and Mary Chaet

*New York • Chicago • San Fransisco • Lisbon • London
Madrid • Mexico City • Milan • New Delhi • San Juan
Seoul • Singapore • Sydney • Toronto*

The *McGraw·Hill* Companies

Copyright © 2009 by Mike Chaet, Ph.D. and Stephen C. Lundin, Ph.D. All rights reserved. Printed in the United States of America. Except as permitted under the United States Copyright Act of 1976, no part of this publication may be reproduced or distributed in any form or by any means, or stored in a database or retrieval system, without prior written permission of the publisher.

1 2 3 4 5 6 7 8 9 0   DOC/DOC   0 1 0 9

ISBN: 978-0-07-162487-9
MHID: 0-07-162487-2

McGraw-Hill books are available at special quantity discounts to use as premiums and sales promotions, or for use in corporate training programs. To contact a representative, please visit the Contact Us pages at www.mhprofessional.com.

Library of Congress Cataloging-in-Publication Data

Chaet, Mike.
  Loops: the seven keys to small business success / Mike Chaet and Stephen C. Lundin; with Vince Moravek and Mary Chaet.
   p. cm.
  ISBN 978-0-07-162487-9 (alk. paper)
   1. Small business—Management. 2. Entrepreneurship. 3. Success in business. I. Lundin, Stephen C., 1941-II. Title.

  HD62.7.C435 2009
  658.02′2—dc22   2009008585

Mike
*and I have witnessed the
remarkable courage demonstrated
by a few of our friends and family.
Sandy Griswold and Janet Hay contracted
the most lethal form of leukemia. And Bill
McClusky, Augie Nieto, Bruce Thompson, and
Al Dykehouse contracted ALS—a disease for
which there is no known cure—in the prime of
their lives. This book is dedicated to them and
a portion of our income and energy will be
directed to those who are working to
cure the disease that has no
alumnae association,
ALS.*

CONTENTS

CONTENTS

ACKNOWLEDGMENTS

From Steve:
I want to acknowledge my wife and best friend, Janell, whose wisdom and serenity have touched many, including our six children, 10 grandchildren, and one great grandchild.

From Mike:
When I thought about writing my acknowledgments I was immediately struck by how many people it takes to bring a book to life. It is with great humility that I attempt to thank everyone who had a hand in this project. Before I name some of you I would like to apologize to those of who I have not directly named but have had significant influence on my personal and professional life and thus, on the final book.

ACKNOWLEDGMENTS

I would first like to thank all of the TEAM LOOPS from McGraw-Hill who have brought this project to life. Ed Chupak for the guidance and leadership, Daina Penikas for her patience, Malvina D'Alterio who did such a great job on the cover art, Jim Madru for his sharp pencil and well used eraser, Maureen Harper, Heather Cooper, and finally Herb Schaffner who first believed in the project.

Second, I would like to thank my great friends and mentors who have taught me so much, Duke Llewellyn, Stephen Covey, Mark Davis, Dennis Dallas, Alan Glick, Gloria Lambertz, George and Barbara Chaet, Patch, John McCarthy, Augie, Mike Van Diest, and all of my students at Carroll College. I would also like to thank Dr. Kim for introducing me to my great partner and coauthor Steve Lundin, for without him this book would never have been written.

And finally, for the support, love, and the contributions to LOOPS of my great and patient wife Mary—she is the essence of LOOPS—and to my four awesome Montana kids, they make it all worthwhile. To all of you a warm and grateful thanks.

INTRODUCTION

Together, Mike and I have been engaged in business pursuits for over a hundred years, including his lemonade stand. We have started businesses, run businesses, invested in businesses, been employees of businesses, buried businesses, taught in business schools, conducted business seminars, made films about business, written numerous books and hundreds of papers about business, developed dozens of business plans, read thousands of books and articles about business, listened to hundreds of talks given by business experts, managed business schools, and generally enjoyed the world of business. We are a couple of business guys. While experience is no guarantee for wisdom, we do have a lot of real-world experience. It will be up to you to decide about the wisdom.

Business has permeated all parts of our life. When we took our young children to their activities, along the highway, we would drive by some businesses with corporate logos recognizable anywhere in the world and countless others much smaller in scope. We always made a point to tell our children that these businesses were not deposited along the highway fully grown. We would emphasize that at some time in the past, all these businesses started with an idea and hard work. We would tell them that not all good ideas came to life as businesses but that those that did were represented by the buildings and logos we passed on the highway Did I say we love the world of small business?

We have observed something about the business world. It was an easy observation because our businesses have been small businesses. Our observation is that most of what is written in business literature is written about big business, the global Fortune 5000. The CEOs of Disney, Mercedes, Boeing, and Sony are more likely to be pictured on the front of *Business-Week* than the owner of Bob's Steak House, Lundin & Chaet Accounting, or Melissa's Meats. And when a well-known business speaker comes to town, you can expect the examples used in the talk to come from large businesses with global reach.

Not only do Mike and I think that small business is more interesting, but we also think that it is more understandable. It is hard for the average person to understand how the mighty Bear Stearns disappeared from the face of the earth, along with a few of my invested dollars, after 70 years of existence and a stellar reputation. The end of Bear Stearns requires understanding complex financial instruments that even the executives of Bear didn't understand fully. The end of Joe's Meats, however, is much more understandable, and the average person is more likely to identify with Joe than with some anonymous and overpaid big company CEO.

We have observed something else: A majority of jobs and most of the new jobs are created by small businesses. The largest segment of the business world gets the least amount of attention.

And we have noticed that all large businesses started as *small* businesses. So you might say that all business, at one time or another, was small business.

If you are an executive of a company with turnover in excess of a billion dollars, you should put this book back on the shelf and find something recommended in the *Harvard Business Review*. If you run a department of a few hundred people inside a large business, you may find a few tidbits here not covered by your extensive corporate training programs. However, if you work in a small business with less than 50 million dollars in sales and with limited resources for the training and development programs big business takes for granted, this book's for you.

Our story unfolds in the context of a family-owned health club business. Mike has built a small but global health club consulting business, and I work out, so we know this industry well. Leadership, management, customer service, marketing, maintenance, motivation, morale, purchasing, finance, operations, human resources, branding, sales, and recruitment are all important to health clubs. In other words, to be successful as a health club, you need a broad base of business knowledge. So a health club is the perfect setting for us to explore the world of LOOPS.

IMPLEMENTING LOOPS IN SMALL BUSINESS

After you have read each chapter and pondered the points following each chapter you are ready for the real work, implementation. You will find follow-up work divided into two categories: "Follow-up Work and Discussions" and "Loops to Close for Your Business." You may want to develop your own protocol, but if not, the following is a protocol that our clients have found useful.

- Call a loop meeting. The attendees will be your decision.
- Choose one of the seven essential loops and read the introduction.
- Have a brief discussion about the loops in the book highlighting key points.
- Go through the discussion topics spending 10 to 15 minutes on each.

- Develop action plans from the Loops to Close list.
- Identify those who are accountable for the actions to be taken, the loops to be closed, and describe what success looks like.
- Review results at the beginning of the next meeting.
- Continue the process for as long as it takes.
- Congratulations! You are now working in Loops Groups.

PART ONE

THE JOURNEY BEGINS

Just as all business starts as small business, all business leaders start as students. We must never lose the openness to surprise, discovery, and adventure we had as young students.

Last Day of Class

Tony Simms was restless. At the front of the classroom, the good Professor Davis was working hard. It was the last class session of the school year, and ahead were finals and a full three months to do something other than sit in classes, read books, write papers, and take tests. The students in Entrepreneurship 101 were ready to escape, and the good professor was trying to make a few final points by summarizing the highlights of the semester's studies.

LOOPS

The students were unaware of the fact that their final exam would leave many of them with their mouths hanging open. It would be a final exam unlike any they had ever taken. Professor Davis wondered how it would be received.

This last class in entrepreneurship wasn't going well at all. The students seemed preoccupied, perhaps thinking of their summer jobs or the looming increase in leisure time. They were entrepreneur students after all, perhaps more wired for action than for sitting.

Tony's mind was contemplating an old issue. He was finishing his third year at Carroll College, majoring in business, and for three years he had wondered why he was in school and not working full time in the family business. He was having those same thoughts today, even though it was the last day of class.

His mother reminded him often that it was his dad's wish that he be the first in the family to get a college degree. So here he was, a good student, but he wanted to be somewhere else. He reminded himself of his personal commitment to make the most of his time in school regardless of his preference to be working. But his mind wandered anyway.

Is this really what dad wanted? Mom is certainly capable of running the show; she's been doing that successfully since dad died and was his partner before the accident. But I know I could be of more help to her. I'm not sure that dad thought about this. Did he anticipate that she would double the size of the business? I could be working full time and taking courses on the side. I enjoy learning, but I should be helping mom.

The sound of chalk against slate drew Tony back to attention, and he read what Professor Davis had just written on the board:

THE CUSTOMER IS ALWAYS RIGHT

"The business world is full of aphorisms. This statement is perhaps the most common. *The customer is always right.* But in business school we try to look beyond the obvious and think for ourselves. Is this statement true?"

Half a dozen hands went up.

"Simms?"

Tony wasn't surprised when Professor Davis called on him for a seemingly obvious answer. He knew Tony was having trouble deciding on a topic for his senior thesis, and there was the fact that Professor Davis had been a lifelong friend of his dad and was scheduled to be on that ill-fated chartered plane three years ago for their annual fishing trip to Canada. Professor Davis's wife, Betty, got ill, and he reluctantly decided to skip the popular annual fishing trip and remain at home. Tony had a vivid memory of his dad reassuring Professor Davis and telling him, "There's always next year Rob! You take care of Betty."

LOOPS

"True," Tony replied after a slight pause, "and *not* true. Because even if he's wrong, it accomplishes nothing to make her wrong, so he is right." Good-natured laughter filled the room at his wise use of gender.

"Clear, concise, and whimsical as always, Tony," Professor Davis said. "Care to elaborate? What happens when it's obvious to everyone that the customer is wrong?"

Tony thought about how he had seen his father and his mother handle customers at the family chain of fitness centers.

"It's not that the customer is really always right. It's our *predisposition* that the customer is always right. It's with that predisposition that a good businessperson approaches every customer interaction. And if the customer turns out to be wrong, we still try to make it right."

Tony continued, "There is, of course, one big exception. The customer is *not* right if she or he is acting in an abusive, crude, or offensive manner with an employee or another customer, even if he or she is right about the issue. Abusive customers we can do without because our employees are our first customer."

"Spoken like someone who has spent some time in the trenches," chuckled Professor Davis. "What does Tony mean when he says the employee is the first customer? Ping?"

Ping paused, and with a quick movement of her head, she tossed her luxurious black hair back so that her face was fully visible, smiled, and responded, "First, I want to compliment Tony on his sensitive nature when it comes to the role of women at work. I am sure that all the women in this room deeply appreciate his use of language . . . and would like to know him better." With that she glanced at Tony with a faux temptress smile, and Tony turned a bright shade of red.

Tony and Ping had known each other since grade school, and their rivalry followed them to college. Lately, Tony had felt completely outclassed by Ping on several occasions. This was one of those occasions.

Professor Davis commented quickly, "Ping. I know it's springtime, but could we get back to the point, please?"

"He means that if we want to take care of customers, we have to take care of those who take care of customers. I remember seeing a film about Southwest Airlines, and the president of Southwest at the time, Colleen Barrett, was real clear about this point when she said that *employees are our first customer.*"

"Thanks, Ping. You've said it well. Our employees are our first customer," and the good professor went on to further illustrate this point and bring the class to a close.

The customer is always right, thought Tony, after being momentarily distracted by the comments of his long-time friend and rival. How many times had he heard that? Hundreds? Thousands? It must be the most universally accepted truth in business.

LOOPS

That's when it hit him: He had never heard his dad say those famous words. Why? It seemed odd that he had never heard them uttered by his father, one of the most successful businessmen in town?

But Tony knew the answer immediately. Anthony Simms, the "Club King," didn't go around spouting aphorisms about the customer being right because *he didn't need to.* It was deeply embedded in his business DNA, and he modeled it in his every customer interaction. There was never any question about his beliefs because they were reflected in his actions.

Again his attention returned to Professor Davis as he announced, "I have a little surprise for you. There will not be a typical final exam for this class during exam week."

There was a smattering of applause and a couple gasps.

"But before you get too excited, there *will* be an assignment in its place. Let me explain.

"When you return from the summer, you'll be in your senior year and facing the need to complete a final thesis before graduation. Our business school has built a reputation for being practical and real-world-based. We'll talk theory, but not without a full dose of reality to make the medicine go down.

"A large number of you have not yet filed your senior thesis topic, and those who have filed have for the most part proposed topics that lack a little . . . how shall I say this? . . . *passion*. So I made a proposal to

the dean a few weeks ago, and he supported it enthusiastically.

"I have prepared a final exam that at the same time
will allow you to make some progress on your thesis.
Here's your assignment. You have all summer to complete it. I look forward to seeing all of you in the ad-
vanced entrepreneurship class in the fall, and I will
collect your assignments then.

"And remember the choice you always have in my
classes. You can do the assignment to get it done, or
you can do it in a way that serves you as a developing
entrepreneur. It can take about the same amount of
time either way, but in the first case you get a grade
and in the second case you get something that lasts a
lifetime. Make this assignment work for you! Well,
enough lecturing for one year."

"Dr. Davis!"

"Yes, Bob?"

"I need to have a grade to get my financial aid for
this semester. An incomplete doesn't work."

"Hmmm . . . good point, Bob. I forgot to mention that
part of the plan." Davis's eyes gleamed. "I'm giving
you all B's. Unconditionally. Why? Because you've all
shown that you deserve that grade, or better, based on
the excellent work you've already completed. But to
have a shot at an A, you'll need to do the assignment."

Bob frowned. "But . . . then why do the assignment,
Professor? I mean, if it just means that you have a
chance to get an A, and without any guarantee at that,

or to have a stress-free summer, why do the assignment? It really doesn't seem like a difficult choice. No disrespect meant, Professor, but is there a trick here?"

"No, Bob. No trick. But, as you might guess, there *is* an embedded lesson here. This is a class in entrepreneurship, and one thing we can't really cover adequately with lectures and readings is the importance of being proactive. Not everyone can do that, but it is important to success in business. Not everyone is wired to go into business for himself or herself, and that's okay. There are plenty of good jobs in big business.

"We're all different in the way we're wired for business. Some of us won't be happy unless we're calling our own shots, and some of us would rather work for someone else.

"I believe that this assignment is the most important assignment of your business school life. Whether you do the assignment or not, you'll learn something important about yourself. The assignment may not affect your grade, but it *will* affect your education.

"With this assignment, you'll come face-to-face with something important to all entrepreneurs—the internal motivation needed when you are in business for yourself. An important part of your education is what you will learn about yourself as you weigh the options."

With that, Professor Davis distributed and quickly reviewed the final assignment. After answering a couple of technical questions, he simply declared, "Have a great summer!" and left without another word. Not a student moved.

Finally, Bob spoke. "This is too weird. I'm going to accept my B and enjoy my summer. Why not? See you guys in the fall."

Final Exam for Entrepreneurship 101

1. Find a respected and successful businessperson, and learn as much as you can about his or her success.
2. Summarize your findings in no more than 12 type-written pages.
3. From the success attributes you identified, choose the one that interests you the most, and summarize this topic in one or two pages. This is the topic of your senior thesis.
4. Bring the result of your work with you to Entrepreneurship 102.
5. Be prepared to discuss what you learned about yourself and your personal decision making.
6. Have a great summer! Feel free to call me if you need to discuss any aspect of the assignment. Whatever you decide to do is okay. There are no tricks. If you don't come with a topic, I will assign you one without penalty.

Professor Rob Davis 224-8723

LOOPS

The students left in small groups, talking quietly as if they were in the library or a museum. Two of the students were already thinking of the assignment as an opportunity.

As the room emptied, Tony decided to go directly to Professor Davis's office. Most of his classmates were aware that he knew Professor Davis personally, but he didn't want to make too much of that fact with anyone but Ping. She was so competitive that he liked to use his personal relationship with Davis to goad her.

But Tony had an odd feeling about the assignment, and he instantly knew *whom* he wanted to study. But there was a problem. And he wanted to talk about it with someone who surely understood.

"Nice surprise," Tony remarked to the professor as he walked though the open door of the office and greeted the man who was like an uncle to him. Then he noticed that Ping was already there, sitting in the big stuffed chair in the corner.

"Hello, Tony. Would this be a good time to get to know you better?"

"I'm sorry. I can wait in the hall."

"Ping and I were just taking care of a loose end." And with that, Ping stood and left the room. As she passed Tony, she smiled. "Have a good summer, Tony. And don't be a stranger."

Tony came into the office and sat down in the warm chair.

"The assignment is fascinating."

"Yes. You probably see your mom's handprint on this assignment. Mary is always bugging me about making my assignments practical. 'Use the real world as your classroom,' she frequently suggests when she gets into her lecture mode. 'Send me graduates who have some practical sense,' she says. And I certainly agree. Do you see any possibilities in this assignment?"

"I knew immediately what I want to do . . . but I have a problem."

"Oh? What's that?"

"I want to study a successful businessperson who is no longer living."

"Ahhh. I thought you might go that route."

"I'm not sure how to approach the subject. I can remember a lot, but most of my memories are from my early teenage years. I've learned enough in psychology to know how much my teenage perspective could affect my perceptions and memories. While I want to study my dad, I'm not sure how to proceed because I can no longer talk with him."

With that comment, Tony found it necessary to pause and regain his composure.

"Sorry, Uncle Rob . . . ah . . . *Professor Davis*. Some things you never get over. I miss him so much."

"Take the time you need, Tony. I would like to say that I understand, but I don't because I am not in your shoes. I do know the sadness of losing my best friend. I can only imagine. . . ." They sat in silence for a moment.

After a moment, Tony said, "Do you see my problem?"

"I do. I think your mom can be of considerable help, though. She should be able to identify those individuals your dad respected. That group of businesspeople could hold some answers for you."

"Good advice, Uncle. Thanks for the time."

"I'm here when you need me. So . . . it sounds like you're going to do the assignment."

"*Absolutely*. I want to help mom with the business, but I'm sure I can find a way to complete the assignment too. See ya!" And with that, the son of the Club King headed for his car.

An Unexpected Meeting

Tony pulled into his driveway and was surprised to see his mother's car. As he walked along the side of the house to the kitchen door, he could see his mom at the table. *What the heck is she doing home during business hours?* He immediately recognized that as a silly thought because their clubs were open from 5 a.m. to midnight.

"Hi, Mom. Are you all right?"

"Right as rain, Tony. How does it feel to be just about finished with your junior year?"

"I had a few surprises today, but . . . are you sure that you're okay? You're always at the club this time of day."

She smiled. "Didn't they teach you about delegation in business school?"

"That they did, Mom. But you and dad *also* taught me about being present and visible in the business 24/7."

"Perhaps we overdid that a little. Anyway, I wanted to be here to talk with you about your surprise. Let's say I had some inside information about the assignment."

"So you and Uncle Rob talked about the so-called exam. Why doesn't that surprise me?"

"And have you decided what you're going to do with this final assignment?"

"What do you mean?"

"Are you going to take the easy B and sunbathe at the beach, or are you going to accept the challenge?"

Tony laughed. "I *am* a bit pale and sure could use some sun. But I'm also excited to take on the challenge. And *yes*, I have chosen my subject. Picked someone immediately."

"Anyone I know?" Her proud look said it all.

"Oh, I think you know him *quite* well, Mom. Give me a hug before I start blubbering for a second time today!"

After a few warm moments, she held her son so that she could look at him, and blinking back tears, she said, "My dear, y*ou're* the reason I'm home. I thought we could use some privacy if you wanted to talk about this unusual final exam. I think it could be a great way for you to prepare for your future, whatever it holds. What are you thinking?"

So Tony told her how Professor Davis had suggested he might study the businesspeople his dad knew and respected as an indirect way of studying his dad. When he was done, he asked, "Will you help me put together a list?"

"I've already started, son. And I have a few ideas that might make the assignment more useful to you as you prepare for your place in this business." She passed him a piece of paper.

Wide-eyed, Tony looked up from the list. "My, you *have* been busy, Mom. I suppose I'll need to share my grade with you.

"Only if it is an *A*."

"Do you think you'll be able to identify someone for each category?"

"Your dad knew a lot of people, Tony. And he seemed to attract the best because he recognized and respected the best."

"These categories remind me of dinner-table discussions. I grew up thinking everyone had family dinners where they sat around the table and talked about business stuff. Now I realize how special that was."

"Family dinner was a priority for us. And it also kept us sane. It's too easy to let a business consume you."

Tony's Summer Job

Divide the summer into seven blocks, each one focusing on one of the business practices that are key to our success.

While studying each subject, work in a related part of our business.

Interview someone your dad respected for each of the seven practices.

The categories I have identified are

- Customers
- Culture
- Fundamentals
- Process standardization
- Innovation
- Real world
- Leadership

And have some fun along the way!

Love,

Mom

"Speaking of business, what exactly am I going to do for you this summer while I'm working on the project? It looks like I'll be moving around."

"Definitely. You'll experience the business at the entry level of every major department as you study the subjects on the list."

"Come on, Mom! I know more about the club business than most of the employees who work for you. I've been in it my whole life, and believe me, picking up towels and cleaning restrooms is the bottom. About as 'real world' as you can get."

"No doubt what you say is true. But you've experienced those things *as the Club King's kid*, and if you'll pardon the pun, you were treated with kid gloves. Now it's time for you to feel the true pulse of the business. I want you to see the business with a fresh set of eyes."

"I suppose that couldn't hurt."

"It's what your father would want."

Tony knew from experience that the subject was now closed.

"When do I get the list of people to talk to?"

"When you finish the rest of your exams next week and have properly celebrated the end of another successful school year, we'll get started."

"You should be a college teacher, Mom."

"Funny you should say that!" She brightened instantly, "I am thinking about applying to become one of the online instructors at the University of Phoenix, where I earned my MBA."

"You would be great. So . . . what's for lunch?"

"Whatever you can find, Tony. I need to get back to work. There's a business to run!"

The Summer Plan

Tony finished his last exam on Thursday morning. The room was stuffy, and someone, probably Ping, was wearing some really annoying perfume. But he was finished now, and he sure didn't have to concern himself with stuffy classrooms, strong perfume, *or* the irritating Ping. He headed for Simms Fitness to get his plan for the summer. He couldn't remember a time in his life when he was more excited about an assignment. Something about following in his dad's footsteps really filled him with energy.

"Hi, Mom. Reporting for duty! I want to celebrate by getting at it."

"You sure you don't want to lie on the beach for a while?"

"I think I would rather get started. Is the list ready?"

"I made the last arrangements just this morning. Walk with me to the photocopier so that I can copy your schedule for the summer."

As they walked to the machine, Tony saw his mom's secretary, Clara, smiling oddly at him. She winked at Tony as they passed, saying, "I gave up asking a long time ago."

Tony smiled back politely, but he didn't understand the comment. Once out of earshot, he asked about it.

"She means that if I was any kind of a *normal* boss, I'd shout out, 'Clara, get this copied for me, please!'

Then she would walk into the office and ask *how many* copies and *when* did I need them? I wouldn't hesitate to do that if I really needed help. . . . Well, I might not *shout*, but I want her to know that I respect her and am not too important to take care of myself.

"We have different jobs, but we're both human beings. So, when I can I make my own copies and get a little exercise to boot, I choose to do it. Make sense?"

Tony grinned knowingly. "And you count every step on that little pedometer of yours and round off to 10,000 steps at the end of the day, right?"

"I do 15,000 steps now," said Tony's mom. "I put on a couple pounds."

Tony had never thought about the nuances of something as simple as getting a copy made. He was beginning to understand what it meant to be seeing the business differently. He was no longer the club rat; he was a colleague.

When they returned to the office, Mary handed Tony his copy of the schedule.

Tony sighed deeply, finally glancing up from the list. "So! Looks like summer will be one big party. Thanks for limiting my time in maintenance to a week. I think I paid my dues there already."

"If you were meant to party all summer long, you'd have been born into another family."

Tony wisely decided not to pursue this comment. "Are they expecting me at the front desk today?"

Weeks 1 and 2: Beyond Customer Service
Assignment: The front desk
Model: The Lava Java

Weeks 3 and 4: Build a Winning Culture
Assignment: Personal training and human resources
(HR)
Model: The Regency Star Hotel

Week 5: Remember the Fundamentals
Assignment: Loop Groups
Model: TFG

Week 6: Standardize Key Processes
Assignment: Operations
Model: The Chicago Sentinel

Week 7: Innovate
Assignment: Maintenance
Model: The Silver Plate

Weeks 8 and 9: Live in the Real World
Assignment: New club opening
Model: Physicians Clinic

Weeks 10 and 11: Leadership
Assignment: To be determined
Model: To be determined

Week 12
Wrap up.

"They are now that you are here, Tony, and they've been told how important it is that you have an *employee* experience as opposed to a *club rat* experience. But I'm not quite finished." Mary hesitated. Took a deliberate breath. "This is hard."

Tony sat down when the tone changed. "What's hard, Mom?"

"At this point in a perfect world, your dad would talk to you about his pet subject. I'm not sure I can do it justice."

"He would lecture me on the importance of relationships, wouldn't he? He was always talking about relationships."

His mother looked more carefully at him. "Yes. Yes he would, Tony. He prized his relationships and called them the most important thing in life outside of family."

"What would he say, Mom? I know he would be sure to talk to me before I started this journey."

A Conversation with Dad

"Yes, Tony. He would say, 'Tony, you're going to visit some very savvy people in the next 12 weeks, and you're going to be a representative of this family as you work with them and as you interact with the employees of their business and of our business.'

"He would go on to say that there's one backbone fact to keep in mind: 'Your mother and I believe that *relationships* have been—and always will be—the heart of our business.'"

Tony nodded as his mother spoke these words. He recognized the ideas from his years as the Club King's son.

"He would tell you that the key to these relationships is what I called 'the magic question': *How can I help you?*

"In the beginning, the magic question was, *How can I help you get into shape?* But, as time passed, we learned that that question had much broader applications. For instance, after we helped our members get on the right track for their health and fitness, we saw that we could expand that concept into the community. Let me tell you a story you're too young to remember.

"Back before the mall was built, there was a big warehouse across the street from our first fitness center. One day that warehouse caught fire. Several fire companies responded, and it turned out to be a day-long battle. You should have seen it . . . fire trucks, equipment, and firemen everywhere. There was barely enough room in the streets for them all.

"It didn't take long for your dad to track down the commander and ask him that magic question, *How can I help you?* Five minutes later, they were using our parking lot as a command center. We even ran out a set of phone lines to supplement their communication equipment.

"Then your dad decided to ask the magic question again. Sure enough, the firemen were eternally grateful to have us open up the lobby and showers for them. Gave them a place to cool down and clean up. Since then, we've had no-charge, courtesy fire inspections, free smoke detectors, and the fastest response in the world if our alarms ever go off. That was not our intention—to get free stuff—but it speaks volumes about how much they appreciated the magic question."

"That must have been hard, Mom. I understand and agree with everything you've said."

Tony headed for the door.

"There is one more thing Tony."

"What would that be?"

"You are the heir apparent of Simms Fitness. Everyone will be watching you to see what kind of person you are. The impression you make is critical."

"Any advice?"

"Be yourself, learn as much as you can, and respect everyone as an equal."

"I will do my best, Mom."

PART TWO

THE SEVEN ESSENTIAL LOOPS

Let's pause for a moment and talk about the idea of loops before we continue the story.

Small business is about getting things done. It makes no sense to purchase an inventory system if you don't install it. It is a waste of time to install it if you don't use it. Purchase, installation, and implementation are three loops, each of which needs to be closed before the business can benefit. Success in small business is about *closing loops*.

L⊙⊙PS

LOOP ONE

Manage the Experience Zones[1]

Customer retention has more to do with making an emotional connection with customers than good customer service. Of course, having both would be ideal.[2] To achieve either, you must know and understand the "experience zones" of your business.

Tony found himself working the front desk during the first week of his summer vacation. Nowhere in the club system is there a greater density of customer service opportunities than the front desk, and by the end of the week, Tony was sometimes wondering whether the customer was really always right.

He almost lost his composure on Friday when a young woman asked him what the club was going to do about her broken nail. Apparently, she had gone to have her nails done on the way to the club, and while using the Precor elliptical machine, she broke a nail. Surely that was the club's fault, she insisted. Tony didn't have a clue as she stood glaring in front of him. It seemed so bizarre that he wondered if it was staged.

At that point, Bill moved over and smoothly became a part of the conversation.

---

1 The experience zones are the places with the greatest density of customer contacts. Steve has written extensively about this subject, and many of his thoughts can be accessed by going to www.topperformer.com.

---

2 Gallup Organization finding.

"May I make a suggestion?" Tony backed up a step to make room for Bill's wheelchair. "Our broken nail policy has been revised recently, and if you come to the desk after your shower, we will have arrangements made for a quick nail replacement."

The woman was clearly surprised by this turn of events. She looked at Bill quizzically.

"Really?"

"It's standard procedure for broken nails. Come to the desk after you clean up, and we will have arranged a place to fix that nail at our expense."

She smiled uncertainly and headed for the locker room.

Bill got on the phone. After one call, he had confirmed arrangements at Moon Nails, literally around the corner.

"Thanks, Bill. I didn't know we had a policy for broken nails."

"We don't, Tony." Bill chuckled, smiling like a Cheshire cat. Sometimes you just have to see the humor in a situation like that and go with it. We could have argued. We could have told her she was being silly, which she certainly was. But where would that have gotten us? She was upset, and we had a chance to make a connection with her by solving the problem. The woman who owns Moon Nails teaches Pilates for us. She was only too happy to help."

When the woman came back, Bill had prepared a little card for her to take to Moon Nails for free replacement of one nail. He let Tony present it to her, and Tony made a small bow as he made the presentation. The woman—feeling ever so sheepish now—simply nodded and headed for the door. At the threshold, she turned and smiled. "Thanks. You guys are great."

After she was out the door, Bill turned to Tony. "She won't forget that." We have made her day brighter from the seeds of disaster. Your dad used to call those 'vision moments.'[3] And he would refer to this front desk as a major 'experience zone.'"

"Vision moments? Experience zone?"

"We talk about our vision of how we want our clubs to be, but until we actually *act* on vision moments, it's simply words and good intentions. The vision moments bring the vision alive. And the experience zone is simply a place where a significant number of customer experiences occur. There are an above-average number of opportunities to make a connection with our customers in one of the experience zones. The front desk may be the largest experience zone in the club. We can do a lot of good here if we're alert to the vision moments."

"How did you even *think* of something like a fake club policy as a vision moment?"

Bill thought for a moment. "When your dad hired me five years ago, he impressed on me that we don't just talk about serving customers at the club, we are

---

[3] Steve first used the term *vision moments* in his book, *FISH Sticks*. The term refers to the building blocks of life that actually create the vision in the minds and hearts of customers and staff.

obsessed with serving customers. And I work in the club where your mom has her office, and I see her spreading the same message. It's fun looking for ways to surprise and engage our customers. They come into the club tired and stressed, and I have a chance to make their day a little brighter. Not a bad deal. I sort of make a game out of searching for vision moments. And I find I've gotten pretty good at it, . . . and it makes me feel good about what I'm doing."

Tony found that his days at the front desk with Bill passed quickly as they searched for vision moments and served customers enthusiastically in the club's major experience zone.

That weekend, his mom told him that the first visit was all set for Monday.

Monday morning dawned bright and clear, the air tinged with anticipation. Tony's mom was off to work early, and Tony could sleep in because he was told that the best time to visit would be 9:30 to 11 a.m. He still didn't know where he was going.

The Lava Java

The note from his mom said simply: "Lava Java." In case he was still sleepy, his mom had left two clues. An old lava lamp and a coffee cup with an address circled with black ink. No chance for a mistake here.

Tony knew enough about Lava Java's many commercials to put it together: His first lesson awaited him at the Lava Java coffee shop at the mall.

L∞PS

Covington Mall consisted of about two dozen small shops strung out between a pair of big-box department store anchors. A wide range of middle-class sedans, SUVs, and minivans in the parking lot meant a thriving flow of customers for late morning on a workday.

Lava Java was as busy as the rest of the mall. Outnumbering the usual mix of coffeehouse patrons was a large number of young professionals. Staffing was plentiful, with two people handling registers and customer lines and another pair cranking out the orders. One thing for sure: Lava Java ran a smooth assembly line of constant customers.

The efficiency of the workers kept the lines down to an average of two or three people with little to no waiting time beyond what it took to prepare the particular orders. Tony thought to himself, *No need to search for the experience zones in this business. There is one big experience zone at the counter.*

Figuring out which of the four workers might be his contact wasn't too difficult. Three of the employees were young, college-age kids like Tony. The fourth, who was his father's age, stepped up to the counter when he saw Tony approach.

"Here, I'll help this gentleman." He smiled wide at Tony, eyes glancing up and down as if measuring him for a new suit.

"Hi. I'm looking for . . . "

"Wait! Lemme guess!" He cut Tony off with an enthusiastic wave and a theatrical fist-below-chin scowl as if Tony were a complex math problem. "Young guy. Studious. Polite. Hmmm . . . you look like an espresso man."

"Well, actually, I . . . "

"No! Not espresso. Too much punch. You . . . you're a *regular* coffee man. And I mean regular. No fancy lattes or fritz mixes. Just a Styrofoam cup filled with heat and caffeine. Well?"

"On the nose!" Tony said. "How did you . . . "

"How did I know?" The man shot a furtive look to each side, leaning forward over the counter to whisper his reply. "Part of the magic. I'm William Alphonso Tiberius Crane . . . but please . . . call me Bill. You're Tony, right?"

The other workers filled in seamlessly while Bill walked out to shake Tony's hand. "Nice to finally meet you! My wife and I met your parents many years ago, and our families have stayed in touch. He caught himself. Yikes! Scary to think about that much time zooming by!

"Let me introduce the team on the fly. Margo, Roberto, and Matt, take a bow." Margo and Roberto looked up and smiled at Tony, but Matt was working with a customer, and he kept his attention focused on his customer, who was talking to him.

Then Matt looked up and said, "And I want you to meet our outstanding customer, Molly, without whom we would all be poor."

LOOPS

Molly looked at Tony with a shy glance and finished her purchase. You could tell she enjoyed the repartee.

Bill picked up the earlier theme of the conversation. "Matter of fact, I think the flagship club was one of my first contracts back when I had my own construction company. Crane Construction put in those very first racquetball courts. And later did those . . . uh, *controversial* remodels that turned the racket ball courts into yoga rooms."

Tony had to laugh. Many times he had heard the story of his mother's insistence on embracing innovations, such as installing the city's first real racquetball courts and, later, the first space dedicated to yoga. His father was often cautious, especially when there was a large expense, but after seeing how successful jumping on the right new trends could be, he always paid special attention to his wife's ideas.

Bill nodded. "The whole experience of working with your dad and mom taught me a couple very important lessons too. Why don't I just go about my business and let you figure them out for yourself?"

Tony got it immediately. "Mom wouldn't want the lesson to be *too* easy, would she?"

"Of course not. So make yourself comfortable, enjoy your coffee, and watch the action."

Tony wasn't sure what he was supposed to see. A steady flow of customers came and went, each taken care of with courtesy and efficiency. Tony did observe that Lava Java had very reasonable prices. On a break between customers Tony mentioned this.

"You're right. The market *does* show that LJ's prices a little below market, especially in this neighborhood. That's part of our strategy, but the biggest part of what your dad would want you to learn here remains to be discovered. Watch us a little longer."

Tony watched Bill and crew service more customers quickly, politely, and efficiently. No, it was more than polite. Tony noted that there was authentic engagement with customers. The counter staff joked, laughed, and seemed to deliberately try to draw at least *some* kind of a reaction out of even the most morose or distracted coffee drinker.

Watching Roberto deal with a mother and daughter confirmed Tony's impression that the staff had made a commitment to engage each customer, not just to serve them.

Mother and daughter were young, mom no older than Roberto, with little girl clinging to her dress. Mom had ordered a Mocha Magma for herself, and while Bill did the mixing and steaming, Roberto turned his attention to the little girl.

He leaned over the counter to establish eye contact. "And you, miss? Nothing on the menu looks good?"

The little girl blushed instantly, moving behind mom and peeking around mom's skirt. Shy, but it was easy to tell that she was intrigued by the attention.

L◯◯PS

Her small cherub face appeared long enough from behind the skirt to exclaim that coffee was *icky*. She added, "My name is Tammy, and I'm four."

"Maybe you just haven't seen our kid's menu." Tammy perked up at the mention of a kid's menu.

Once sure that he had her attention, Carl picked up a blank order sheet and looked at it intently. "Wow, look here! Today, a special on broccoli lattes! You like broccoli, Tammy? We also have tomato coffee."

Tammy let out a, happy squeal, aware that she was being teased. As mom got her Mocha Magma and moved off with a laughing wave of her hand, the little girl kept turning back, smiling wide with each of Carl's clever offers. It reminded Tony of the club experience with the broken nail.

"Green bean tea? Potatoes on a stick? Wait! Where ya going? There's more!"

As Tony continued to watch the action, he was impressed.

"You engage customers in a personal and authentic way," Tony said to Bill on another break. "Is that a part of what my dad would want me to see?"

"Sort of simple, isn't it?" nodded Bill. "And yet I would say that it accounts for 90 percent of our success. It's not hard to make good coffee and to price it right. It is hard to build a reputation as a place that provides a special customer experience. We pay very careful attention to who we are being while we are doing coffee shop. People come for the coffee, but they come back because of the experience *and* the coffee.

"We also try to know everything we can about our customers. Because we get a lot of health care professionals who work in the hospital, we have a line of coffee drinks with odd names. They love our 'Emergency Room Special,' which has enough caffeine to kill a horse. And we have a line of drinks for the health-conscious."

"Like your Half-Caff menu," Tony replied. "Many of those I saw ordering from the Half-Caff were carrying a gym bag. Health-conscious members of those four health clubs in the area no doubt, one of which carry the name Simms, I might add."

They talked for another hour, Tony filling four pages in his notebook. Meeting with his dad's old friend was like spending time with his dad. He didn't want to stop. As the conversation wound down, Bill looked at Tony and said, "Is this hard? Talking about your dad."

"It *is* hard. But it's also *rewarding*. When I started, I didn't realize just how personal it would be. I'm finding clues to my dad's life in the people he knew and respected, and for that, I am grateful beyond description." Tony paused, smiling through moist eyes. "And you know? I'm really looking forward to the rest of this quest. There will be emotional moments, but I am getting to know my dad in ways that are not only rewarding on a personal level but also educational as I gear up for a life in business."

"Your dad was special, Tony. And this community is better because of him. Say 'Hello' to your mom, and remember, the coffee's always on me."

LOOPS

Tony's Notes on Experience Zones

Experience zones are the areas where a large number of customer contacts occur. You will best manage the experience zones if you

- Identify and understand your true market.
- Study your customers and potential customers until you know them well.
- Find out what customers want, and give it to them plus a whole lot more.
- Separate yourself from the competition through differentiation.
- Make an authentic emotional connection with your customers in the experience zones.
- Engage! Engage! Engage! Create a powerful customer experience with laughter and energy.

Loop One Development Plan

Follow-Up Work and Discussions

1. Reflect on various types of businesses, and share experiences you have had with great management of experience zones while you were a customer. How about poor experiences?
2. List your own business's experience zones.
3. How could you better manage these zones so as to create a more positive or exciting experience for your customers?
4. Describe your business's market area. Detail it geographically. Describe drive-time analysis and general customer demographics. The greater the detail you can provide, the more it will help you to make decisions. Ultimately, you will want to put it on a map.
5. List your competitors within this market area. Provide details regarding their products, service, and pricing that compete with you.
6. Describe how your competitors are managing their experience zones. Describe both good and bad.

LOOPS

Loops to Close for Your Business

1. Answer this question in brutally honest detail: How is your product actually different from that of the competitors in your market area? If you are not different, describe the similarities. How do you compare in the management of your experience zones?
2. Describe how you plan to better manage your experience zones so as to maximize the experience of your customers each and every time they enter each one of these zones.
3. Develop a list of loops to be closed in order to accomplish these goals. Assign them to people, and also assign deadlines.
4. Describe your plan to make your business different from that of your competitors.
5. Imagine your business after this is done. What does it look like to a potential customer?
6. Outline how you can sustain this difference over the next one to three to five years and into the future.

LOOP TWO

Build a Winning Culture

> Employees create a winning culture moment to moment.
> These moments accumulate to build a culture, a brand,
> and a reputation. Vision moments are those conscious acts
> generated from a fundamental commitment to the vision
> of the enterprise. The fundamental commitment guides
> each employee to accept responsibility for recreating the
> vision every day by living the moments.

Tony reported to the human resources (HR) department only to find that the HR director was at another
club conducting performance review training. The
receptionist in HR passed along a message that
suggested that he spend his time with Ronnie, who
was described as one of the most successful personal
trainers.

Tony knew Ronnie by reputation and set out to find
him. After a couple of inquiries on the workout room
floor, he was sent to the Strive Circuit. As he looked
down the Strive Circuit, he saw only one personal
trainer—a woman his mother's age who was enthusiastically guiding a young man through his routine.

What an idiot I am! Ronnie's a woman.

Tony was fascinated by the energy of this diminu-
tive woman; he would later learn that she was a cham-
pion natural body builder in the masters division. As

he watched her work with a client, she was demonstrating, crouching to get a good look at form, supporting, encouraging, smiling, correcting, and all the while dropping priceless bits of information about diet, stretching routines, body carriage, and a host of other topics.

At five minutes to the hour, she shook hands with Julie, her client, and Tony heard her say, "I've enjoyed working with you, and I thank you for your business. Will I see you next week at this time?" She held eye contact with Julie until she turned to go. Only then did she acknowledge Tony.

"Hello, Tony. I only have five minutes to take a bite of my energy bar and prepare for the woman warming up on the treadmill. Why don't you just tag along as my partner? You've spent enough time in the gym to know a thing or two."

Tony arrived home that night completely exhausted from being Ronnie's partner, and after trying unsuccessfully to watch *24*, his favorite TV program, he went to bed early.

Tony didn't get to Ronnie, personal training, HR, or anywhere in the club the next day because, at dinner the night before, his mother passed him a matchbook from the Regency Star Hotel as he dozed at the table. As his curious head rose, Mary told him about his appointment for the next day.

Regency Star

At 9 a.m., after a sound night's sleep, Tony arrived at a huge glass skyscraper in the heart of downtown Chicago, where his contact would be Wayne O'Brien, the Star's current catering director. Tony felt a bit silly pulling up in his Mini Cooper and parking behind a late-model Mercedes. He had barely gotten out when a polite, impeccably uniformed valet appeared. Without any sly, sideways glances at his jeans and tennis shoes or any other hint of patronization, the valet treated Tony with genuine courtesy and respect.

Well-dressed guests, visitors, and support staff bustled through a busy lobby roughly the size of Grand Central Station. The front desk was a gorgeous wonderwork of polished wood, brass, and gold inlays.

As per instructions, Tony marched right over to the first check-in line, trying to pretend that he did this sort of thing all the time.

Only one person was ahead of him—a businessman in a well-tailored suit with a cool leather briefcase at his feet. Tony guessed that this wouldn't take too long; all three front desk clerks in sight zipped credit cards and sales slips about like the blackjack dealers he remembered from his one trip to Vegas with his dad.

Unfortunately, in Tony's line, nothing seemed to be moving. Seconds later, the distressed voice of the man in front of him grew loud enough for him to hear.

LOOPS

"Oh, that's just *great*. What the hell am I going to do *now*?"

Uh-oh. Trouble in paradise? Tony followed the exchange between clerk and guest like a verbal tennis match, pretending to be completely absorbed in a blank notebook page and hoping they wouldn't notice his interest.

"I don't believe this. I'm literally out of options."

"Perhaps not, sir. What again is the length of your . . . er, *package*?"

"Main crate? Talking a square, solid 10 feet each side. Then there's four smaller ones, but each at least six feet by six. Won't be fitting into any hotel shuttle van. If it wasn't for this brutal deadline, it wouldn't be such a big deal!"

"Yes sir, they *are* big. You say it's imperative that they all travel together?"

"Can't deliver pieces."

"I understand. I can't believe there's not another suitable transport vehicle in downtown Chicago. The concierge is on his way, and if anyone can help . . ."

"Thanks, anyway, but unless it happens within the next few minutes, I'm afraid it would just be too late. May as well delay my checkout time while I call some freight companies. Geez! You'd think the museum would send a better truck in the first place. The First Emperor's warriors should rate first class!"

Had Tony not been so puzzled at that last sentence

that he actually whispered "First Emperor's warriors?!" like a shocked little kid, he might have realized sooner that his eavesdropping had been noticed.

Both men stared with arched eyebrows, but Tony could only shrug. "Well, sorry . . . but that isn't something you hear every day."

It turned out that Tony had heard right. The "businessman" was actually an archeologist associated with the Far East studies department of a Kansas City art gallery, and he was, indeed, escorting imperial warriors. "They belong to the Terra-cotta Warrior Museum in China," he explained. "And one broken-down truck is bringing down the whole chain of delicate flight connection schedules designed to get these artifacts back to Shaanxi Province in time."

The desk clerk leaned forward across his polished counter, gesturing toward a big, disheveled man in work overalls approaching the desk. "Gentlemen, this is Mister Maxson Slater," said Eddie, the desk clerk. "He works for a local hotel supply firm, one to which we give our highest recommendation. And he happens to have a Kenworth Freightliner flatbed tail-up to the loading dock as we speak."

Long after truck driver and archeologist disappeared into their own personal history, as Tony was waiting in the lobby for O'Brien, a tuxedo-clad young man—apparently the concierge—showed up at the desk to hear the story. Their conversation looked almost *too* animated, as if they were discussing a thrilling football game or action blockbuster instead of a simple example of fast-thinking, exceptional service.

Later Tony found out why. The Regency Star staff actually held a running *contest* to see who could upstage the other in the customer satisfaction department! More amazing, this "contest"—although sanctioned by upper management—was something completely originated by hotel staff. That was one way to make sure that the magic question is never forgotten, Tony wrote in his notebook moments before Wayne O'Brien arrived for their appointment.

O'Brien took an immediate interest in the various comments Tony had written in his notebook. "Empowerment, eh?" O'Brien burst into laughter. "Holy crow, boy. Your mom's going to be mighty pleased to see how you figured most of it out before I could get you out of the lobby!"

"Eddie's a perfect example of empowerment," Tony said. "In the 10 minutes I've been here, I watched your desk clerk handle several awkward situations. Just minutes ago, a sour couple who'd been arguing since getting off the elevators started complaining to Eddie. I realized the complaints had nothing to do with the hotel when I heard the lady complain that the shower water was both 'way too hot' and 'way too cold.' They were just complaining to complain, but Eddie gave them a 10 percent across-the-board discount on their final bill."

O'Brien took the news with a nod and a smile. "Yes. They're allowed up to 15 percent on their discretion. We build our culture around empowerment and great service."

"That doesn't surprise me at all," Tony responded. "The lesson I will take away is one of allowing your employees to make command decisions for on-the-spot solutions."

"Of course, the whole staff empowerment element has to have a foundation of well-trained, competent employees. Then you supercharge your staff. Let them find the answers, close the loops. We base our training on accountability, thus ensuring that our people define and take responsibility for the specific *who, what, when,* and *where* of all tasks. The results are amazing. The entire operation becomes all about the people—truly an awesome force."

Wayne O'Brien still had plenty to show Tony as they toured the big hotel, moving through public areas and staff-only behind-the-scenes service passageways.

As the catering director for a large hotel, O'Brien dealt with hundreds of different organizations, associations, corporations, groups, and individuals who sought out the Star's 16 different meeting rooms and convention halls. O'Brien and his many assistants booked the rooms, negotiated the contracts, laid out break and meal menus, arranged audiovisual and electronic equipment and furniture layouts, and oversaw essentially every other detail that successfully pulled off a myriad of seminars, workshops, weddings, reunions, dances, ceremonies, buffets, and more.

All routine stuff for the intrepid catering department, but the key element O'Brien wanted Tony to see was so subtle that he had to point it out. It had to do with the role of communication.

"I'll explain how important this is." O'Brien stopped in at one of the back supply shelves and demonstrated with real-life examples. "We send booked organizations these special confirmation packs. The confirmation packs provide the feedback that allows us to make the *exact* number of meals.

"All organizations," he said, "are able to estimate their attendance pretty well if you stay with it. A few good ones already had their ducks in a row initially, but usually that isn't the case."

O'Brien's office had a small department devoted solely to confirmation data. The staff worked with the booking organizations to get firm feedback for those perfect numbers long before the event occurred. Staff members never waited for someone to "get back to them." They e-mailed. They phoned. They sent funny greeting cards with stamped reply cards. They wanted every loop closed on every attendee and each speaker. It was all worth the effort when individual cost figures for each attendee might top a thousand dollars.

"This communication focus is important to any business. Whenever you want to communicate a message, do so in a way that both serves the organization by securing the information needed to plan effectively and leaves the lasting impression that you have been in touch with a special place—the Regency Star. Every part of this organization from housekeeping to catering has a role in maintaining the high standards we set for ourselves and in developing an incredible culture."

"May I have a copy of your guiding principles to take with me?"

Wayne grinned, "I only have a few hundred copies left, but I suppose I can share one with the son of the Club King. As a matter of fact, it's my understanding that your dad sat with my predecessors some 20 years ago and made a similar request."

Tony said his goodbyes and headed for the lobby. Passing through the lobby, he veered left to the front desk and thanked the staff for the earlier lesson. There was still a buzz at the desk, and the word of their coup was continuing to spread throughout the building.

As Tony headed for home, he was deep in thought. *Our personal trainers have the most contact with customers and are crucial to the lasting impressions a customer forms. Front desk personnel are also a high-contact area. Are we as thoughtful about the culture we develop as the Regency Star? Do we need to be? What is the extent of our empowerment? Isn't empowerment sort of like freedom? Why don't we just say freedom?*

On the seat beside him sat the core principles of the Regency Star.

L⌾⌾PS

Tony thought of one he would add to his list: I am dedicated to acting on the vision moments with which I am presented.

Keeping his eyes on the road, he thought about the items on that list. Those principles are day-to-day tools with which to build a culture.

During the next few days, Tony learned a great deal about personal training and actually had a few opportunities for hands-on. He was always conscious of Ronnie when she was in the workout room with a client.

---

[4] These are taken from the Ritz Carlton's 12 service values, as presented in *Human Resource Management Singapore* 6(8):27, 2006. The Ritz Carlton has a vision of "ladies and gentlemen serving ladies and gentlemen."

He saw her introduce clients to each other. She always had time to greet people as she guided her client from machine to bench to machine, all the while encouraging hydration. Ronnie's enthusiasm was infectious, whereas many of the other trainers he met and worked with seemed to be simply going through the motions.

On the second to the last day in his rotation, Kim Beasley, the HR director, finally showed up and found him on the floor. "Do you have a moment, Tony?"

"Huh? Oh, hi Kim. I do. How was your training session at the Elgin Club?"

"It was great. I'm so new here that I had trouble just *finding* the club. Elgin is like out in the country. Come in and tell me what you've been doing."

Tony described the front desk, personal training, and his visit to the Regency Star. He decided to share his concerns about the personal trainers.

"Kim, I can't help noticing the big difference in personal trainers. You have Ronnie—who fills the room with enthusiasm and seems to be building a community—while all around her are these bland associates going through the motions."

"There's no test here, Tony, but if there were a test, you would have passed it with flying colors. When I was hired, personal training was one of the key issues. Did you meet the head trainer?"

"No."

"That's because we don't have one.

"I like to think of HR as the department that takes

overall responsibility for building a culture. Simms Fitness will not reach its full potential until we get greater consistency on the gym floor."

Later, Tony ended his rotation realizing that the gym floor was yet another important experience zone with hundreds of potential vision moments every day. He thought about this. *In order to build the culture we desire at Simms Fitness, all these vision moments must be acted on. They are like open loops waiting to be closed. Open loops waiting to be closed. . . .*

Tony's Notes on Culture

Vision moments are the building blocks of a culture. They are also the building blocks of the brand.

The set of principles I received at the Regency Star help to explain the hotel's success.

Empowerment is the freedom to make things happen for customers and colleagues when needed.

The workout room is rife with vision moments lost.

HR can orchestrate the building of a culture, but everyone in the business must be involved and committed to execution.

Vision moments are like open loops waiting to be closed.

Loop Two Development Plan

Follow-Up Work and Discussions

1. Discuss the vision of your company.
2. Describe some typical vision moments a customer may experience when coming in contact with your business.
3. Describe how well you are doing in your business with these vision moments and how they could be improved.
4. Describe your current culture. Is it where you want it to be?
5. How can we ensure that vision moments will be handled as a top priority at our business?

LOOPS

Loops to Close for Your Business

1. How well do you do with vision moments with your staff? Your customers? Your vendors?
2. Describe how you plan to improve the delivery of your vision moments so as to make each one a "blue ribbon" vision moment.
3. How would you measure success or failure in this area?
4. Put your plan into written format.
5. Imagine your business after this is done. What does it look like to a potential customer?
6. Outline how you can sustain this new level of engagement over the next one to three to five years and into the future.

LOOP THREE

Monitor the Fundamentals

There are certain basics in every business. All businesses make assumptions, establish direction, set goals, assign responsibilities, measure accomplishments, track progress, communicate results, and make necessary changes. And while these basics at times can seem routine and perhaps uninteresting, they must be monitored continuously. Fundamental loops must be constantly and continuously closed.

Tony took his mom out to dinner on Friday night. He talked about his observations in the workout room and how he felt that a lot of opportunity was lost. She listened intently. Then she filled him in on her two biggest challenges in personal training—turnover and a general shortage of well-trained professionals.

"Tony, I think our new HR director is the right person to make progress in this area. She understands the importance of the issue, and she's a sharp one. Let's put culture building aside and talk about your next rotation.

"A number of years ago, your dad and I invited a small group of local business leaders to a meeting. We were having some problems, and they all stemmed from not paying enough attention to the fundamentals. It is so easy, especially with someone like your dad, who had so many ideas, to lose sight of the basics. And we got so involved in neat new stuff that we forgot about the fundamentals, and it almost cost us the business."

The Fundamentals Group

"During that time, we were in training at the church to become facilitators for a support group the church was planning to create for parishioners who were out of work. As a result of that training, we had become aware of how important support groups could be for people.

"We decided that we needed a support group to keep us focused on the fundamentals. So we invited a group of businesspeople we respected to join us at a monthly meeting. We began by holding the meetings at the university because Rob was our first facilitator. We called it 'The Fundamentals Group,' or 'TFG.'"

"Professor Davis was a participant? Is he still involved?"

"He comes to occasional meetings, but the first thing he helped us to see is that we needed to take responsibility for the meetings ourselves as a part of our own personal development. And, as usual, he was right. We have all learned a great deal about running a meeting and dealing with conflict and the like."

"Cool."

"There are more than a dozen businesses involved. They include a car dealership, a dental practice, an accounting firm, a hotel, a restaurant, a window cleaning franchise, a bank, a real estate office, and a small division of General Motors. Membership requires more than showing up. Each member is expected to actively participate in what you might call homework.

"Each of us in The Fundamentals Group has taken the time to craft our vision for our business and share it with the other members. We have each developed and shared our goals, guiding values, action plans, and the metrics we use to measure progress. We make regular reports on the progress made on key metrics, and we discuss challenges with the group. It is one of the best things we have ever done.

"At our meeting we also have an educational experience, and we take turns locating speakers, 'Webinars,' and other educational activities."

"I knew about the meetings, but I didn't realize you were also going to school."

"And it's a great school. TFG lives entirely in the *real world*, Tony. We're talking about our livelihood and the source of income for those we employ. There's no lack of interest. We're all motivated and engaged because it's our *life*.

"Monday I want you to come with me to the meeting. I'll pick you up on my way downtown, say, about 9:30."

"Sounds great. I think I learned more in the last few weeks than I learned in a whole year of school, and this looks like another great learning opportunity. And it's practical! Not academic."

"Both are important, Tony. There is a place for each. You and I lean toward the practical, but I believe that we each value the academic as well. By the way, I am really enjoying this process. It has stimulated me at a time when I needed stimulation. It is so easy to get in a comfortable rut. And it's fun to 'hang out,' as you young people say."

TFG Meeting

Tony and his mother arrived at the midtown bank precisely at 10 a.m. The guard recognized Mary and smiled. Mary chatted with her for a minute, and they then proceeded to a wood-paneled conference room that was already full. Mary took the remaining spot at the table, and Tony sat in one of the chairs that lined the wall. As Mary sat, she gained the group's attention and introduced her guest. "Hi everybody. This is my son Tony, who you so graciously allowed me to bring today. I have briefed him on what we do here, and he will observe as a part of his summer internship experience."

A number of the participants nodded, and those close by offered a quick handshake. At the end of the table, a man stood.

"My name is Ralph Witherbottom. I own the Witherbottom Cleaning Company, and I'm the designated chair. Welcome Tony. Hey, why don't we make room at the table for Tony?"

After everyone was settled, the members went around the table and reviewed their milestones for the past month. A few described activities that were initiated during the month. The general manager of Hola Tex Mex reported on an improvement in the process by which the company purchases its raw materials that resulted in a reduction of waste product production of 15 percent. As the members went around the table, a lively discussion sometimes would follow the update; at other times, the members simply would go on to the next person. Every presentation included a statement of progress on key business goals.

On the ride back to Simms Fitness, Tony couldn't stop talking. His mother rarely saw her son so animated. *If he can get this excited about the basics, he should do well in business.*

The Loops Group

As they pulled into the parking lot, Tony asked about his Simms assignment for the week. "I'm not real clear about my assignment this week. On the schedule it says 'Loops Group.' What in the world is the Loops Group?"

"That you will see in a few minutes. Follow me."

"What about lunch?"

"All taken care of, Tony. Do you really think I would let you starve?"

LOOPS

Tony followed his mother up the back stairs to the Simms conference room. As he entered, he longingly eyed the sandwich buffet. The buffet was crowded, and most of the club's managers were filling their plates. His mother turned to him, "The Loops Group is our version of the TFG. I figure that if it does me so much good at the corporate level, it ought to be useful at the department level. We have been doing this for only four months, and the managers love it. Say your hellos, and listen in."

Tony had just begun his greetings when Charles Anderson, the manager of development, called the meeting to order. Tony scrambled to make a sandwich as the meeting got under way.

He quickly observed a similarity to the meeting he had attended in the morning. Each department presented the goals being highlighted and the metrics being monitored. Occasionally, another manager would ask a question or observe an important connection to the goals of another department. This would lead to a short supportive problem-solving discussion. Tony felt a sense of pride because the meeting was every bit as rich as the one he had just attended. *This Loops Group is full of positive energy. Funny, but I don't recall any mention of fundamentals groups in my classes other than quality circles. I think the energy is a result of discussing things that are real and important.*

Tony and his mother left the room after an intense hour. "So what do I do with the rest of the week?"

"You will love this part, Tony. It is a license to learn. I want you to visit with each of the members of the Loops Group and have each person explain his or her vision, goals, and metrics. I want you to develop a thorough understanding of how each member sees his or her job and what each considers important. Go to it."

Tony's Notes on TFG

A group of committed businesspeople can help each other succeed.

Working on fundamentals is an ongoing activity.

The group makes the fundamentals more interesting. When you present your business results to a group of peers who are dedicated to your success, good things happen.

There is always energy when you work on real stuff.

The Loops Group produces an energy that is natural.

LOOPS

Loop Three Development Plan

Follow-Up Work and Discussions

1. Discuss why you would join an *external* group of noncompeting diverse business owners.
2. Describe why you might wish to form *internal* loop groups within your company.
3. List the fundamentals and issues common to all businesses.
4. List issues that you would like to have *internal* loop groups work on.
5. Where would you find one or more of these *external* loop groups?

Loops to Close for Your Business

1. Ask around to see if any *external* loop groups exist. Look into joining one.
2. If they don't exist, how could you start one?
3. List the first five questions you would like to present to the *external* loop group.
4. List the issues in your specific business and one major issue you would like to start your *internal* loop group working on. Start the groups.
5. Set a schedule for your *internal* loop group to meet.
6. Do it!

LOOP FOUR
Standardize Every Major Process

One of the greatest inventions in business is the standardized process. Without a standardized process, each event would be treated as novel, and very little would get done—and what did get done would be inconsistent. Standardizaton and systems helps you close loops in a predictable manner.

Tony woke to the sound of his mother calling out, "Coffee's on, and information about your next visit is on the table. I am leaving for work."

Tony stumbled into the kitchen and picked up the note. "Your meeting is at 10:30, so read the paper. Have you visited your dad lately?"

The only thing on the table was the *Chicago Sentinel* newspaper. He would read it later. His mom had reminded him of an important family ritual.

So Tony started his day in his dad's office. As he opened the door, he steeled himself for the emotion that was certain to follow. As he entered, it was immediately reassuring to see that the walls were still covered with memories. Everything was the way it was on the day his dad had died. His mother had decided to leave it that way.

There were framed letters and poster-sized banners declaring their club's first open house. A hundred photographs, glossy prints, grainy newspaper black and whites, and assorted items were so dense that they became a collage. Tony took it all in.

The club's first dollar bill was displayed in the wall's center. Postcards from members, staff, or vendors filled all the empty spaces. He thought to himself, *Good morning, Dad. I miss you, and I plan to make you proud.*

He had noticed it before, but today it really struck him. In almost every picture, his mother stood beside his father. *They had always been a team. I wonder if I will find someone to be my partner in life.*

Tony returned to the kitchen and picked up the paper. For a moment, he was irritated to find himself wondering about Ping's summer. He opened the paper to see a big red arrow pointing to a specific underlined name on the staff list. Tony was obviously supposed to visit Gladys Thornby, production manager. "10:30 a.m." was written in red.

The Chicago Sentinel

Tony should have looked more closely. Gladys Thornby was difficult to locate. After showing up at the *Sentinel*'s downtown editorial offices, Tony was redirected halfway across the city to the paper's new printing and distribution facility in Oak Brook. By the time he found his way through a sprawling industrial park, he was over an hour late. He took a seat in the facility's bland lobby, where the constant thump of nearby machinery could be heard and felt.

Gladys seemed to take his tardiness in stride when she appeared a few minutes later. Their introductions included a surprising story of how she had been one of the very first people to sign up for a Simms corporate club membership. In fact, Tony had seen a picture of her on the wall in his dad's office that very morning. Her youthful, fit appearance showed that she took advantage of membership.

"Not surprised you went downtown first. Half of metro Chicago doesn't even know we exist!" Gladys Thornby didn't exactly *yell*, but she wasn't soft-spoken either.

"How's your mom?"

The question caught Tony by surprise mostly because the woman seemed all business. He managed to say, "Great. Thanks for asking."

Gladys kept talking as they zipped down the plant floor in a golf cart, staying between two yellow stripes.

The next 45 minutes were a dizzying tour of hanger-sized rooms filled with mammoth, ear-splitting machinery. Miles of pipes stretched in every direction.

"Ink," said Gladys pointing at the pipes. "We use offset techniques for full-color printing, which uses a planographic printing plate—a plate with dual sections, each chemically different from the other. The nonimage areas are attracted to water, whereas the image areas are attracted to oil. An oil-based ink wets the image area, whereas a water-based fountain solution wets the nonimage area. Simple, huh?"

Tony listened politely to these details but began to wonder what he was supposed to learn.

"Finished products are bundled, loaded, and trucked to satellite distribution centers throughout the metro area, where, ultimately, local carriers deliver the paper to merchants, coin boxes, or the paperboys who toss it in your driveway. The paper is on time because of one big system. Everything is systematized."

Gladys lead Tony into a small break room. They sat down at Formica tables, and Tony was grateful to finally pull off the heavy ear protectors. "So. What do you think? Learn anything useful on my little tour?"

"One thing is clear: The process I just witnessed seems *impossibly* complex!"

"The process is complex because you are inside one of the systems. If you were inside the system that places a call you make on the phone, it would seem just as complex. On the outside, however, you place a call and calmly wait for an answer. It works time after time. On the outside, it seems simple.

"But that is not the main thing you are here to see.

"The newspaper that was delivered to your door, hopefully on time, is the result of three basic systems: *writing*, *printing*, and *delivery*. Our part is the printing. The three connected systems create a larger system that delivers the paper to your door on time, day after day, year after year.

"And no system's worth anything without the proper quality controls. The individual steps require *some* supervision, or you risk compromising the final product. But the reason you are here is simple, not at all complex. Without systems, this would be an impossible task. The standardized systems allow us to operate on a large scale and meet deadlines all along the process.

"When your paper is late, what part of the process do you think is usually responsible?"

"I would guess delivery."

"Exactly, and why is that."

"Well, writing is done by professionals supported by technology they use every day. Printing is a function of keeping the machines operating, and that too is done by professionals. Delivery is subject to a sick driver, traffic, weather conditions, and a host of other variables that are hard to control."

"I see the apple hasn't fallen too far from the tree."

They talked for a while longer. Gladys told Tony how she met his dad as they drank undrinkable coffee. The last words Gladys said kept playing in his mind: *What standardized systems allow Simms Fitness to operate at scale?*

Simms Operations

Tony reported to the club manager of the Elgin Club the following day. He carried with him the final question asked by Gladys. So when he sat down with the club manager, Tina McPherson, he began there.

"Mary told me a bit about what you are doing, Tony. How can I help?"

"I am trying to understand the nature of the standardized systems at Simms and why they are important. Yesterday I visited the *Chicago Sentinel* printing plant, and it is easy to see the systems in action and why they are important. It is not so clear to me why they are important here at Simms."

"Why is that?"

"Well, we have customers, and customers need individual attention, not a script. It would seem, for instance, that a system guiding customer service would feel artificial to the members."

"Think about the writing part of the *Chicago Sentinel* system. Do you think that the editorial writer has less freedom in choosing a subject because he has a deadline?"

"No. An editorial writer wouldn't tolerate anything that affected freedom of the press. I see your point. The writers operate freely within a system that has deadlines."

"Lets take a walk." Tina directed him to a spot near the front desk and said in a quiet voice, "Let's just watch for a while."

After a couple dozen members came and went, she pulled Tony over to an unused membership desk, and they sat in the two chairs located there.

"What did you see?"

"Members arriving and checking in and members leaving."

"And how does the system control the behavior of the front desk person and the member?"

"Everyone needs to register."

"And where is the freedom that is similar to the freedom of the editorial writer?"

"Has anyone told you that you would make a good university professor?"

Tina smiled, "Not recently. Question too tough?"

"Fortunately, I have already spent some time working at the front desk. I think the freedom is in the greeting and the interaction that takes place while registering."

"Has anyone told you that you should be a student."

"That I hear all the time."

"I'll bet you do. What else did you observe?"

"Some of the members were there for personal training, and their check-in took a bit longer. Afterwards, they received a receipt."

"Right. And what is the system behind that receipt?"

"I think they sign up for a number of personal training sessions. The larger the number of sessions, the greater is the discount they receive per session. The receipt is evidence that one session has been consumed."

"Exactly. And the payroll system updates the account of the personal trainer and the member. Can you imagine what it would be like if all these things happened by word of mouth. Suppose that a member comes in, has a session, and the personal trainer tells the front desk to make a note of that. A lot of clubs operate that way."

"I see the point. The trainer might forget to get it recorded. It also would make it possible for a trainer to take cash, overcharge, or otherwise abuse the system. Or should I say, the lack of a system."

"Most of our trainers are men and women of integrity. The system isn't a judgment; it's simply good business. Sort of like the teller at the bank counting the money twice and checking your ID before allowing you to cash a check. The system protects the business and builds in reliability."

"Got it."

"There are a couple of related systems that you might find interesting. Every new member goes through an evaluation and is offered a free personal training session. The focus of that session is to get started on things identified in the assessment. A by-product is that each member becomes aware of the personal training services available.

"There is also a system we call the 'We care about you system.' If a member goes three weeks without coming into the club, a phone call is generated. We know that members who haven't used the club in a while are most prone to drop out. So a call is made, and they are asked if the club services have been satisfactory and if the club could be of help getting them back on their program. After the call, a T-shirt is sent to them that reads, 'I Work Out at Simms.' The personal touch makes all the difference."

"Who makes those calls?"

"I do. It may be the most important thing I do. If you remember my presentation at the Loops Group, I monitor this factor closely. Now let's take a look at the cleaning system."

"I have some personal experience in this area. It is the natural home of a club rat with a dad like the Club King."

"I didn't know your dad, but from what I have heard, it isn't surprising that you have spent some time cleaning locker rooms and picking up towels. Let me take you through the system that ensures satisfied members. Having a clean club is critical to member satisfaction."

Tony's Notes on Standardized Processes

At the club we have standardized systems for membership, billing, maintenance, cleaning, and new club openings.

The system does control the behavior of those who use it but leaves a lot of room for individual expression.

Maintain quality control at all levels.

Every big job is the combination of many small jobs.

For a big loop to get accomplished, the small loops must be closed first.

L⬮PS

Loop Four Development Plan

Follow-Up Work and Discussions

1. Discuss with your staff why standardization is important in your business.
2. Make a list of high-leverage management activities you would like to be doing that you do not have time to do because you are too busy doing daily stuff.
3. List the areas in which you have positively applied standardized processes in your business.
4. List the areas where you need help.

Loops to Close for Your Business

1. Make a concrete list of processes that need standardization.
2. Research how best to get this done (internally or outsourcing).
3. Evaluate how much time this will free up for either you or your key people.
4. Calculate the cost versus the return from increased productivity.
5. Set your priority list, with the most profitable at the top of the list.
6. Standardize the first item on the list, and work your way down.

LOOP FIVE

Innovate

"Grow or die" is often misunderstood as a philosophy. It does not mean always get *bigger*. Size is the least important dimension. It means always get *better*. Standing still is a sure formula for moving backwards. Whether you call it *kaizen* or *continuous improvement* or some other name, innovation must be a key ingredient in any business.

Tony had been told to wait at home for a phone call, so he quickly picked it up when it rang.

"Mister Anthony Simms Junior, please."

The voice on the other end was stiff and formal. Tony pictured a butler.

"Speaking," Tony replied, suppressing a chuckle.

"Mister Simms. My name is Thaddius Hoff, chief host at The Silver Plate. I'm to confirm your ten o'clock brunch appointment."

Tony was impressed that his dad had known someone at the most exclusive restaurant in town. But a glance at the clock suddenly put the invitation in a different perspective.

"Uh, yes. . . .Did you say 10 o'clock? I'm way out here in Hillsdale, so I better get going. What's your address? I've never been . . ."

The chief host interrupted politely but firmly. "No worries, sir. If I may be so bold as to suggest that you look out your front window. I believe our car is waiting for you as I speak."

"A car? No kidding!" Tony could imagine stiff Mr. Hoff wrinkling up his nose at such foolishness as he jumped up and peeked through curtains.

A sparkling white limo waited in the driveway.

Tony raced for the door, scooping up his trusty notebook on the way.

He arrived at The Silver Plate to discover it wasn't even open for business. The place was a chaotic construction zone! Behind a curbside sea of pickup trucks, electrical vans, and other vehicles, workers swarmed the site, carrying tools and lumber.

The driver spoke, "We've reached your destination, sir. I've been instructed to advise you that Mister Hoff will meet you in the restaurant. It's been my pleasure to serve you today."

"Ah . . . yeah, likewise, I'm sure. Did my mom arrange a tip?"

"Gratuities have graciously been prearranged. Thank you for asking, sir."

Relieved because he wasn't carrying much cash, Tony stepped out of the limo and immediately spotted the Plate's tuxedo-clad chief host scowling at some workers—until he noticed Tony, free of either overalls or hardhat—and his expression changed instantly into a wide, professional smile.

"Ah, Mister Simms, I presume? Welcome, sir, you've been expected. Right this way, . . . and please, disregard all the commotion. A disagreeable necessity."

The thump-bang-clunk of construction carried throughout the restaurant during Tony's delicious brunch. He had just finished a heavenly blueberry cheesecake dessert when the waiter reappeared to remove the dishes. The timing of the service was almost spooky—Tony decided that either someone constantly had an eye on him or they had a NASA mission control of monitoring cameras. Sure, he was the only actual diner in the entire restaurant at the time, but he'd heard enough about The Silver Plate to know that this type of exemplary service was standard operating procedure.

"Will there be anything else?" the waiter asked with a cultured smile. "We offer an elegant selection of brews from lattes to fine . . ."

"Hey, truck stop regular's fine. Long as it's hot and has caffeine, y'know?"

Hoff reappeared on cue, perhaps 16 seconds after Tony's last sip of some fancy Euro-brand coffee that was a bit bitter to his uncultured taste but still had plenty of kick. Good thing, too. The chief host was back in disguised drill sergeant mode, acknowledging Tony's gushing compliments while ushering him up out of his chair.

"Splendid! Chef will be pleased to hear the new special gets high praise."

"That's putting it mildly! That honey-glazed meat filet-thing . . . yummy!"

"High praise, indeed."

It took perhaps 90 seconds for Hoff's manner to clue Tony in that his role now was strictly to follow him around. Questions were okay, as long as they weren't too stupid and there weren't too many.

The destination was the staff locker room, where a woman with "Cara Dannon—Dining Room Supervisor" on her name tag was trying to quiet down a crowd of cooks, waiters, waitresses, and other staff. The noise in the crowded room was deafening with the cheerful banter of a carnival atmosphere. "People, please! Settle down!"

No good.

Then Hoff placed a hand on the supervisor's shoulder, gave an exasperated sigh, and clapped twice—*loudly*. Instantly, all heads turned and conversations ended. In a matter of seconds, the locker room was silent (except for the construction noise constantly intruding). All eyes faced forward on a thin-lipped chief host—ample evidence the guy could back up his style: half the busboys weren't only silent but *scared*.

"Ladies and gentlemen," Hoff spoke. "If you could be so kind as to garner your attentions to Ms. Dannon, I believe she has a few announcements about this month's gourmet motifs. Cara?" Hoff stepped back while the dining room supervisor cleared her throat.

"Yeah, thanks, Mr. Hoff." Ms. Dannon shot a glance at the chief host and turned to the assembled crowd. "All right . . . you've all got your new uniforms, and judging by the noise, a positive response?"

Several cheered. Two or three whooped.

Ms. Dannon had her hands up quickly before things

could get too loud again. "Okay, okay. I just want to make sure that we're all on the right track. I see Cody is about finished passing out the theme. Let me just summarize this month's package, and we'll see if there are any questions."

Hoff handed Tony a ledger-size manila file folder labeled, "Gourmet Motif—April: Springtime Skies," and said, "This, Mister Simms, will allow you to follow along."

Tony glanced inside while Cara Dannon spoke, and immediately he began to understand why those who frequented the Plate usually described the experience with words such as *fresh* and *exciting*.

As it turned out, The Silver Plate—already at the top of its category—took its atmosphere of excellence to another unique level. Each month, the restaurant adopted a gourmet motif that added a distinctive, stylish spin to the dining experience.

This "Springtime Skies," for example. The reason there'd been so much noise among the staff was because their elegant, sparkling new uniforms had just been passed out to unanimous enthusiastic approval. Along with subtle decorating adjustments, several menu items also were either added, changed, or somehow tied into the motif, thus justifying the "gourmet" label.

It all struck Tony as pretty clever, offering customers a reliable, high-class experience while keeping it from ever getting stuffy.

"The patience you've shown during the remodel has been fantastic," said the dining room supervisor, her voice competing with the sounds of construction work being done in a far wing of the building. "The crew boss ensures me that they'll be finished and out of there by four at the latest, so tonight promises to be a great debut for the new open-air skydeck dining. You all have your packets. So have a good time out there, and as we like to end all these meetings,"—her tone turned to that of an emcee—"*why* do we do this?"

The assembled staff responded as if they'd done this before, roaring as one:

"*Because there's no such thing as standing still!*"

"Right! Because . . . ?"

"*Our customers are dynamic with dynamic demands! We must change to keep up with them! We must create our own obsolescence!*"

"Yes! And if we won't do it . . . ?"

"*Someone else will!*"

As Tony scratched some notes, the place erupted into cheers and self-congratulations. When the crowd finally dispersed, he eagerly waited for Mr. Hoff to finish some last words with the dining room supervisor before coming back to him.

"That was great! Do I get a tour of that skydeck now?"

Hoff wrinkled his nose. "Certainly *not*. We can't have strangers underfoot at such a critical time!"

Oops! "Sorry, I slipped. Guess I got caught up in all the excitement."

"Quite. Now sir, I believe you've been introduced to all the facts as requested by your mother. Allow me to show you to your car."

Uh-oh. Tony was afraid that he had offended him.

Hoff shrugged off a dozen attempts at apology, asserting no offense at being referred to as the cliché of a butler and even admitting such reflexive characterization was, in fact, encouraged. He said the restaurant demanded that type of effective discipline (although Tony didn't notice anybody else acting like Hoff). At least he *did* explain obsolescence. "Forecasting your own state of being obsolete. To avoid such is to remain new, vital, and exciting to your customers."

Hoff wouldn't hint at his past contact with Tony's parents, brushing his inquiries off with a dismissive, "True gentlemen need not delve into past history to prove a present acquaintance or responsibility."

After ushering Tony outside, where the limo was waiting, the chief host abruptly turned on his heel and disappeared back inside the restaurant.

Tony underlined a single phrase in his notebook as the limo bounced along: *"Innovation is the lifeblood of business."*

And so his week in maintenance took on a whole different meaning. Tony realized that *each* department at Simms Fitness is a source of innovation and that the work of maintenance and housekeeping is visible to everyone who enters the club.

Now, when he looked at the new soap dispensers in the locker room, he saw an innovation that cut costs, improved the look of the shower room, and was viewed as an improvement by the clientele. *Innovation!*

Tony's Notes on Innovation

Innovation is the lifeblood of any business.

Customers are dynamic; they have ever-changing needs.

You are innovating in your business or you are losing ground to your competitors because your good competitors *are* innovating.

Plan for your own obsolescence.

Teach your people the fundamentals of innovation.

Respect all ideas.

LOOPS

Loop Five Development Plan

Follow-Up Work and Discussions

1. Discuss what is meant by the statement, "Plan your own obsolescence."
2. What is meant by "In business, there is no such thing as standing still."
3. List three innovations you have made in the last five years and what effect each has had on your business.
4. List areas in your business that obviously *need* innovation.
5. Now list areas that aren't quite so obvious.

Loops to Close for Your Business

1. Make up a concrete list of areas that need innovation.
2. Now get together with your staff and complete your list with other areas of your business that need innovation.
3. Evaluate how important each is. What is the cost? What effect will each have on your business and your return on investment?
4. Set your priority list and schedule for ramping up these changes.
5. Start with the first item on the list, and work your way down.

LOOP SIX

Live in the Real World

Living in the real world means planning for the unexpected by leaving margins. Plus having a plan B and maybe even a plan C.

The visit to the clinic seemed like it might end before it began. The card Tony had been given indicated a 10:30 appointment with a Dr. Barbara Deininger, so that's when Tony showed up, mindful of how little flexibility physicians' schedules allowed. He felt a little guilty; the overworked woman probably was squeezing him in between real back-to-back appointments.

He had barely announced himself to Ben, a young man about his age who he later learned was the office manager, when the good doctor herself breezed out of the waiting room door and greeted Tony.

"Hello, Tony."

Dr. Deininger was a tall woman, tan and fit like the rest of his dad's friends. If they were all members of his father's clubs, Tony thought, they must use other branches or times when he's not there. He had never seen her before.

Which turned out to be exactly the case. "I hit your Palace Club every day at 5 a.m. before rounds. It's one of the most important parts of my day. And your mother is one of my inspirations."

"I know what you mean. I have trouble keeping up with her in the gym."

No white hospital coat for her; the doctor dressed in casual slacks and blouse. An omnipresent stethoscope reinforced her image and left no doubt that she was still a physician despite the comfortable dress.

"I want to thank you for taking the time today. I can't imagine how busy you . . ."

As if on cue, Dr. Deininger's belt pager chirruped to life and stopped him midsentence.

She laughed. "If not, I'd bet that you're starting to get a good idea!" Dr. Deininger unclipped the pager, checked the numeric readout, and replaced it back on her belt with one smooth, practiced motion. She turned to Ben, expectantly waiting on the other side of the counter.

"That's the ER. They're calling me back in. Kuntzweiler's probably got the MRI results on our peds MVA. Have Dr. Gould go ahead with the 11 o'clock office appointments. I'll call in with an update."

Ben took a clipboard Tony hadn't even noticed the doctor was holding.

"What about Mrs. Nash?" Ben asked. "She won't want to leave until you reassure her about her cholesterol numbers."

"If she wants to wait in Room 3 until I return, that's fine. Make sure that she's stocked with magazines; I'll have the lab shoot the results to me over in emergency. If I can't get back in a reasonable time, I'll call."

"Sounds like a plan, Doctor. Good luck over there."

Dr. Deininger looked pained, but only briefly, and clearly confident of her priorities. "Not too unex-

LOOPS

pected, I'm afraid. But no worries about your lesson plan, Tony. We'll drop back to plan B and let Ben show you a few things. Nice to meet you!"

Dr. Deininger vanished before Tony could say a word.

In the moments before Ben came around to the waiting room, Tony noticed something strange. Four or five of Dr. Deininger's adult patients were occupying the waiting room, all reading magazines . . . or actually *pretending* to read. With typical human nature, many glances went to the exchange between Tony and the doctor, and certainly ears were tuned in. Yet not one person so much as blinked when the doctor ran off. Tony was surprised to see no fidgeting, mutual glances, or deep sighs of resigned frustration. Didn't they realize that they had just lost their appointments? Didn't they know that they'd be waiting another hour or so to . . .

"Mrs. Beckworth?" The waiting room door opened to admit a smiling Mrs. Beckworth as an older, balding man in a white coat and stethoscope came in the front door and followed her. The name tag read "Dr. Gould."

No wonder they weren't worried. All the waiting patients must be here to see this Dr. Gould instead of Dr. Deininger. *Wrong!*

Ben answered Tony's questions as he sat in Ben's office, trying not to get in the way as he moved from filing cabinets to phones. Other staff helped out; nurses and techs moved constantly back and forth through the back corridors and examination rooms.

"*Peds* is a shortened version of *pediatrics*, as in *pediatrician*. Doctor D. isn't actually a pediatrician, but she's had a lot of background training in peds trauma before concentrating on family practice. The ER physician called her in on a general consult because the patient is from out of town, and she's already been called in on the brother. *MVA* means *motor vehicle accident*."

"I hope they'll be okay."

Ben smiled. "Initial reports are really good."

That relieved Tony. He didn't expect this kind of human drama . . . just checkups, sore throats, hangnails, and such. Then reality appeared in the form of the unexpected. "So, if Dr. Deininger never returns to the office, how do you manage all the patients?

"Plan B. Dr. Deininger getting caught at the hospital is something we know will happen from time to time. Nevertheless, the office has to continue to function without a hitch."

Ben explained most of it . . . and clarified a lot more. For instance, nearly all the patients waiting in the lobby *were* there to see Dr. Deininger!

As it turned out, Dr. Gould, Dr. Deininger's partner, was specifically on hand to continue care without skipping a beat. With alternating on-call schedules, their physicians' group acknowledged reality and ensured both ER call coverage and office continuity.

Additionally, half the patients were in for wellness checks or other routine visits. Ben went on to clarify even more.

"Unlike 90 percent of all other doctors and dentists, we do not try to maximize the number of appointments in order to handle a greater volume of patients. We work to maximize the quality of care and the patient experience. Because we do this with great consistency, our patients give us some slack and understand when things get crazy."

Ben continued, his voice full of pride. "Our patients have a 95 percent show rate, and having the on-call doctor lets us see nearly 100 percent of them within five minutes of their scheduled time."

Tony spent the next hour and a half watching people cycle through the process that anticipated real-world events. When he saw everything that he thought he was going to see, Tony flipped over to a blank page of his notebook and made a few quick notes.

One comment that Ben made he tried to recall verbatim: "Successful businesses accept the world for what it is, not for what they think it *should* be."

The visit to the physician's office was well timed because Tony's next rotation was the new club opening team. And there was a club due to open in two weeks. A club opening is a great place to apply lessons about the real world because club openings are always full of surprises.

Tony found that the club opening team automatically built in margins with extra staffing, extra food to back up the refreshments, extra equipment, spillover parking, and contingency funds and contingency plans for bad weather, zoning board delays, and the like. Tony's contribution was a suggestion that staff coverage overlap an hour to allow for communication and learning during staff changes.

Tony's Notes on Living in the Real World

Accept reality. Leave margins in time (and money).

Successful businesses accept the world for what it *is*, *not* for what they think it should be. They close their loops by planning and acting accordingly.

Plan well. Check your progress along the way.

Work within real-world circumstances.

Expect the unexpected.

Understand that whatever happens has, in fact, happened. It can't be undone, only dealt with. In this way, the unexpected is simply material that allows you to show your flexibility and ingenuity.

L⊙⊙PS

Loop Six Development Plan

Follow-Up Work and Discussions

1. Discuss the concept of margins and how margins affect a person or a business.
2. What can be done if a person has to deal with heavy customer traffic on a daily basis?
3. How is working out actually the same as building or leaving margins?
4. List areas in your business that obviously *need* work in the area of margins.
5. Discuss how having a plan B has helped you with a past project.

Loops to Close for Your Business

1. Make up a concrete list of areas and procedures that need greater margins and/or a plan B.
2. Now get together with your staff and complete your list with other areas of your business that need greater margins and/or a plan B.
3. Evaluate how important each is. What is the cost? If there is a cost, what will be the effect on your business?
4. Set your priority list, and schedule training and implementation.
5. Start with the first margins item on your list, and work your way down. Leave yourself enough time to get all of this done well.
6. Review several projects going on in your business that probably should have a plan B. Create such plans as you see fit.

LOOPS

LOOP SEVEN

Lead by Example

> Leading by example sends such a powerful message of integrity and is such a profound source of inspiration for employees that if you can lead by example, the rest of leadership will be a cinch.

At supper, Tony was asked what he planned to do for the last rotation. Leadership had been left up to him because it was assumed that by the time he reached this point in the summer, he would have some ideas of his own. And indeed he did.

"Mom, I think I'll brief you in the morning. I have it pretty well worked out, but I want to sleep on it."

She suggested that he celebrate his successful summer by going out to breakfast and meeting her at a great breakfast place in Oakbrook. She said that they could meet at 9 a.m., after her staff meeting, and that a cab would be waiting for him at 8:30. Tony thought that this was odd, but he was tired and let it pass. The next morning, a beat-up and rusting cab appeared in the driveway.

"Here I am," he shouted to the driver of the cab as it started to back out.

The fiftyish driver, overweight and scruffy, jerked his head in Tony's direction as if expecting a mugger. His surprised curse was colorful, loudly exclaimed, and quite unrepeatable as he impatiently waved Tony into the back seat.

The perfunctory and quite wooden "Hey, Buddy, what's up? We gots to *go!*" turned out to be the trip's conversational highlight. For the next half hour, Tony was treated to a virtual ballad of depressing, unwanted information.

The guy never took a hint, just prattled on, complaining the whole way about the Chicago traffic. In one short ride before the day barely started, the guy managed to totally bring Tony down. If bumming people out ever became a recognized specialty, that cab driver deserved an honorary degree. The driver grunted something that could have been a "Thank you" for his tip, probably unconscious of the fact that he shook his head in thinly veiled disgust, as if fully expecting that this kid would tip him like a successful businessman on an expense account.

Tony hurriedly slammed the door on additional unwanted advice and walked into the club. His mother was smiling at the door of Egg and waiting for him.

He smiled as he "got it." Tony could just imagine his mom setting up this ride with a confused taxi dispatcher: "I'll pay double for Jim. He is without a doubt the worst driver I have ever experienced!"

"Thanks, Mom. That was a real experience—*in misery*. I suppose it was meant to be a lesson of some kind."

As they sat down in the booth to which they were directed, she responded, "The impact one human being can have on another human being is easy to underestimate. One really negative person can drain the energy out of any enterprise. You just experienced one of the most negative people I have ever ridden in a cab with. He is totally dedicated to his negativity.

"Two lessons here. First and most obvious is the insidious impact of a negative employee, competent or not. The second lesson is that, as leaders, our impact is magnified. As a leader, we want to set the example. Have you decided who you want to spend some time with in this last rotation and where in the club you want to work?"

"I have. I want to spend the next two weeks riding in that cab." Tony said this with a straight face, and his mother just looked at him.

Then she broke out laughing. "Touché."

"Actually, Mom, I want to merge my club assignment and my mentor assignment. I want to work as your aid for two weeks and shadow you, helping where I can, but watching you as a leader who does an amazing job of leading by example. I want you to be my mentor in leadership."

"Well . . . I . . . what if . . . when . . ."

"Just say yes, Mom."

"Yes, Son. I am both honored and delighted."

And so the two members of the Simms family spent two full weeks together. It was an experience that they would look back on as a highlight of their life. Mary walked her talk, and Tony came to understand why she was given not only respect but also love.

Tony's Notes on Leading by Example

A leader is constantly being watched by his or her followers. These are a few of the questions those associates are asking themselves about the leader:

- Is he serious about this?
- Does she really care?
- Is this a whim or something important?
- Does she respect me?
- Will he listen to my ideas?
- Does she tell the whole truth?
- Does he have my best interests in mind?
- What are we building together with our life energy?
- How does what we do make a difference?
- Does she follow her words with deeds?
- What does he think of my performance?
- Does she really want to know when something isn't working?
- Is he here for the long haul or just passing through?

LOOPS

Loop Seven Development Plan

Follow-Up Work and Discussions

1. Discuss what is meant by the term *leadership* and *lead by example*.
2. List five key characteristics of a strong leader.
3. What do you think is the best way to develop leaders in your business?
4. Discuss areas in your business that could use better leadership.
5. Discuss how you personally could be a better leader.

Loops to Close for Your Business

1. Make up a concrete list of areas in your business that could use better leadership.
2. Now get together with leaders in your business and discuss how to do better.
3. What will be the real effect on your business?
4. Set your priority list and schedule by which you will accomplish this objective.
5. Start with the first item on the list, and work your way down. Remember, you need to be going first and *walk the talk*!

PART THREE

THE FINAL LOOPS

Sometimes loops can appear unexpectedly and carry a powerful emotional charge. These are the loops you will remember for a lifetime.

Two Meetings: One Expected and One Unexpected

Tony's summer journey had come to an end. There were still a couple weeks before the beginning of the school year, but he was excited to tell Professor Davis about his project and his plan. He gave the good professor a call, and a meeting was arranged for the next day.

Tony arrived at 8 a.m. sharp with two cups of coffee from Lava Java. He was surprised to find Professor Davis already meeting with someone. The laughter he heard told him that the other person in the office was the always-irritating Ping. Tony was surprised to find himself pleased about this turn of events. He had missed his banter with Ping.

"Come on in, Tony. We're just finishing up. Ping was telling me about her summer."

"Hi, Ping. If I had known you were capable of getting out of bed this early in the morning, I would have brought another cup of coffee."

"That's a nice thought, Tony. It was convenient to make an appointment after my morning run."

Stepped into that one, thought Tony.

Professor Davis joined the exchange, "I've already had my coffee, Tony, so please give her my cup."

Ping offered a coquettish smile and a thank you as Tony handed over the cup of coffee. "How sweet, Tony. I hear you've been busy this summer, too . . . not opting for the easy B but taking on the assignment."

"Yes. And you?"

"You know me, Tony. I *love* to work. Hey. I saw you at the Star Regency. Amazing place, isn't it?"

"Yes, I remember seeing you, but I was caught up with my appointment. I hope you didn't think me rude."

"Oh, I could see you were too busy for little ol' me! Well, thanks for your time, Professor Davis. I'll get out of your hair. See you around, Tony! Don't be a stranger."

"Yeah. See ya' around, Ping!" She shot him a brilliant smile as she backed out the room with the second cup of coffee. *Why did she always make him feel so self-conscious?*

"Well, good morning, Mister Simms. Summer is just about over, and we'll be back in class soon. Ping has been busy with her project. She chose to study the president of the Women's Network. How have *you* been doing?"

Tony handed Professor Davis his summer schedule, and for the next 15 minutes, he went through each of the experiences and the corresponding work at the club.

"You've had quite a summer, Tony. I bet you learned more about business this summer than in all the business classes you've taken."

Tony blushed at the truth of the statement and the implication and stumbled a bit saying something about it all being important.

"You don't have to be embarrassed, Tony. The real world is always the place where the most significant learning occurs. I just hope that you noticed the things we talked about in class when you saw them up close and personal."

That statement caused Tony to think. *Would I have had the same experience without the book learning? Did the academic frameworks help me see things more clearly?*

Tony tucked the thought away for a future time and decided to share his most significant observation with Professor Davis.

LOOPS

Loops, A Common Thread

"I think there is a common thread that runs through my experiences. I think it's . . . uh . . . all about loops, sir. Success in business is all about closing loops. The *right* loops, of course."

"Excuse me?" Professor Davis cupped an ear, something he usually did to a mumbling student during class.

"Loops. You know how people say that we need to 'close the loop'? Success is built one loop at a time. Boiled down, cut to the core, it's the single most fundamental element of business success. Closing open loops, Professor. Every one of the people I met with said so in their own way. They were people of action. They got things done. They executed. They closed loops!"

Tony raced on. "Each of the people I met with was selected because of dad's respect for them. They were an impressive group, all successful businesspeople. I was fascinated with their insights into key business practices. While their stories were compelling, I kept observing an underlying *principle* common to them all—that of finding the best way to get things done, closing loops. The ultimate reason they all are so successful is that they knew what was important to the business, and they got it done."

Tony held up his hand, thumbs and fingers curled into a circle. "Loops. Closing the loops in the mind of the customer, closing open loops in systems and methods. Look, I know it sounds strange. Me bumbling on about loops must sound silly. On the surface, it seems so simple. It is simple. But sometimes the simple things are overlooked."

Davis grinned. "Sounds like you're excited about these loops."

"I am excited! And *that* is what I want my thesis to be about."

"Closing loops?"

"Not exactly. I want to actually *close* one special loop that will help me to share the idea loops with others."

"Well, a thesis on loops seems like a logical choice given your revelation. But I'm not totally clear on what you're suggesting."

"That's the one problem, sir."

Professor Davis frowned. "How could there be a problem?"

"I have a special form I would like my thesis to take."

"A special form? What sort of form?"

Here goes, Tony thought.

"As you well know as the first TFG facilitator, mom and dad derived considerable benefit from participating in The Fundamentals Group. So much so that mom has initiated loops groups at Simms. The simple idea is that participants can improve their chances for success in business by meeting with peers and talking about their challenges. In a way, they help each other identify and close the important loops. And they have fun doing it."

Professor Davis responded, "I was involved in the beginning, and they still invite me from time to time when they think I might enjoy the subject or have something to offer. They seem to have expanded into personal development as well.

"In fact, their naturally evolving commitment to learning has led me to dream about organizing something similar for business students, but the idea overwhelms me. There never seems to be enough time to do all the things I want to do as an educator."

"Well, I hope this is good news," said Tony. "That's what I want to do! I want to organize a Loop Group for junior and senior business students. I think that we could find key business leaders in town who would be willing to let us study their businesses, and in that way, we could work with real stuff. I want these juniors and seniors to get a real taste of the business world while learning from each other."

"Well, I'll be," replied Professor Davis. "Perhaps my dream will become a reality after all. Yes, I am vitally interested in your idea."

"I believe I can make it happen, sir."

"So just to be clear. Are you suggesting that I let you *start a club* instead of writing a paper."

"Silly?"

"Unusual, . . . yes. Silly? No. I love the idea, and I'll go you one better. I'll extend the same deal to one other person if you want to recruit someone to help you. It is a big undertaking. I was talking to someone just this morning who just might be interested."

Tony smiled, "She does have a lot of energy."

"May I be your club advisor?"

"Loop closed!" proclaimed Tony.

"There is one more thing."

"Oh."

"Since you won't be writing a paper, I am going to insist on a final oral."

"A final oral?"

"Are we into the echo thing again?"

"What is an oral?"

"A final oral is a chance to defend an idea verbally. A committee is formed called the *oral committee*. You meet with them for an hour or two, and they ask you questions about your thesis. In your case, the thesis would be something like, 'Closing loops is important to business success.' You are not writing a paper, so I want to hear you defend your ideas about loops."

"When would this happen?"

"Midyear. Probably January."

"And who would be on the committee?"

"Creating the committee will be my job, but it makes sense to use the leaders who extended themselves to you this summer."

"It sounds a bit scary, but those who helped me this summer provoked the idea, so that should be a good deal for me."

"I will set it up. Now get to work on this Loop Group."

After Tony left the office, Professor Davis sat in stunned silence. *My dream will become a reality after all. Thanks, Club King. I wish you could see this. Perhaps you do.*

Tony left Professor Davis's office both excited and concerned. The final oral caught him by surprise. *It shouldn't be too big a deal, but I need all the help I can get.*

He stopped in the parking lot to call Ping on his cell phone. She gave him a hard time, but he could tell from the beginning of the conversation that she liked the idea and wanted to participate. He even had an odd feeling that she was expecting the call.

Finally, after doing her cute thing, she purred, "Tony, that's a fantastic idea. And it says something very nice about you. I would love to *partner* with you on this. When shall we meet to discuss our strategy? I am open this afternoon. How about 2 p.m. at the Lava Java near campus?"

Tony didn't notice the use of the word *partner*. And since he also wanted to get started, he didn't notice that his partner was already acting like one. He would have a lifetime to learn the subtleties of communication between the sexes.

Senior Year; Entrepreneurship 201

Tony was halfway through the first semester of his senior year. He and Ping had worked tirelessly to get the Student Loop Group off the ground. There were 12 current participants, and each had a business sponsor. Five applicants were waiting for a sponsor. It was going well.

Professor Davis had asked Tony and Ping to brief students, faculty, and corporate sponsors on their progress. There was so much interest that they had to move to the large lecture room. A number of businesspeople were coming so they could determine if they wanted to sponsor a student.

Professor Davis made some opening remarks and then continued, "You folks can imagine how proud I am of this group of young people! This is an amazing thing for their education, for the college, and for the community. I now want Tony Simms to tell you about the Student Loop Group."

Tony took things in order and described his summer assignment and how he had chosen his dad to study. He explained how his mother had helped him select a group of businesspeople who had a working relationship with his father. He quickly summarized his journey of discovery and expressed his fascination with the concept of businesspeople supporting one another and how he came to the conclusion that it would be helpful for students as well.

LOOPS

Tony decided not to mention loops because that might be confusing. Finally, he summarized: "This summer was a great learning experience. It also allowed me to get to know my father as a businessperson. He was a great dad, and I have learned that he also was a well-respected entrepreneur." Then he paused and looked down for a moment. When he looked up, his eyes were glistening.

"My dad used to talk about the importance of relationships. But I know better now. It was much *more* than relationships. He enjoyed helping other people reach their goals. He took pleasure in lending a helping hand. He loved to extend himself and make a difference. In my own small way, I wanted to make a contribution to honor all that he has done. I wanted to be like dad. And that has a lot to do with my interest in starting a Loop Group for students. But I haven't done it alone.

"I would be remiss if I didn't comment on my amazing partner in this venture. Ms Ping Wang, would you say a word or two? Your energy and intelligence were critical to making this happen."

Ping kept her remarks brief, and when she sat, the applause was enthusiastic. When the applause faded, Professor Davis returned to the front of the room.

"Thanks, Tony, and job well done, Ping. Now we have a small task to perform. Tony and Ping have essentially completed their senior project, and I want to close by evaluating their performance.

"I've taught a lot of students over my career, but I can't remember more than a handful who actually gave something back to the university before they left. That is the true essence of leadership. Leading by example. Well done, Tony. Great job, Ping! You have completed this portion of your senior project *with distinction.*"

The Final Examination

Tony arrived at the conference center located in the student union and sat in the chair placed outside the Windy City Room. He was nervous.

Ping went first, and he expected that she would be finished by now. He hoped that she had done well.

"Your turn in the meat grinder, partner."

He looked up to see Ping standing in the door with an unusually serious look on her face. "Was it that bad, Ping?"

"I am not supposed to say anything to you because our exams are similar. The committee is taking a break, and they said it would be 10 minutes before they start your final oral. Since I can't say anything, I'd better leave."

Tony watched her leave and was once again alone with his nervousness. He became tighter and tighter as he pondered all the things that might go wrong. A few of the committee members came out to use the rest rooms, but none of them spoke. They only nodded.

Their faces were somber. Tony felt his tension rise. *Let's get this over with!* Finally, Professor Davis came to take him into the room.

There was a long oval table in the room with an empty seat at the far end. Tony knew everyone in the room, but Professor Davis went through the formality of introducing him. Then he looked at Tony and said, "Tony, would you please describe your thesis for the committee?"

Tony took a deep breath and began. "I observed something in my summer study of my dad as a respected business leader that I felt was significant. Since many of you were a part of that study, you probably will recognize the ingredient. Much of the success you have achieved seems to be because you execute, you close the important loops. Let me explain."

As Tony continued to describe his loops theory, those assembled around the table seemed rather cool to his idea. There was very little reaction and no smiles at all. Tony found himself talking faster as his anxiety increased. He finished in a rush and sat down.

Professor Davis stood and invited question, saying, "Will the members of this final oral committee please ask any questions you need to ask before determining whether this thesis is worthy of approval."

Wayne O'Brien stood. "Isn't this idea rather simplistic to be considered for college credit?"

Wayne sat, and Tony felt a chill. *This is not going to be the walk in the park I expected.*

"Simple for sure, but definitely not trivial. It is the kind of simplicity you find on the other side of complexity. You have to earn it with experience, but when you find it on the other side of that experience, everything falls into place, and you have a sense of knowing it is true." As he said these words, Tony wasn't sure from whence they came. Perhaps a dinner conversation long ago. He continued until he felt he had said enough.

"Thank you. That answers my question."

The next question came quickly, "Is this your work, or is it your dad's?"

"Both. My task was to study a leader, and I chose my dad. In that sense, it is his work." Tony chanced a smile. "But it was a lot of work to discover what made him a successful businessman."

Tony waited for the next question. And waited. And waited. Finally, after an uncomfortable period of time, Professor Davis excused him by saying, "I guess the committee is ready to make a decision. Tony, would you please step outside and wait for us to complete the formalities. We will then invite you back in and communicate the final decision after our discussion."

Tony left the room and shut the door. Ping was sitting in one of the chairs.

"I thought I would give you some emotional support. That is an intense experience. Say, I saw your mom downstairs."

"Thanks, Ping. I'm afraid I blew it in there. As I described my findings, I detected no support at all for the thesis about loops. It was a disaster. And they only asked two questions!"

Tony looked down the hall to see his mother approaching. He stood up and gave her a hug. "I've blown it, Mom. What are you doing here?"

Before she could answer, the door opened, and the somber atmosphere inside had been replaced by something now more like a party. The committee was lined up at the door, and as Tony went down the line, it was less of the gauntlet he expected and more of a pep fest. Each member of the committee shook his hand and said some version of, "Good job, Tony."

Professor Davis was at the end of the line. When Tony reached Rob, he said, "Does this mean I passed?"

"Yes. In fact, that decision was made some time ago. You might liken today to an innocuous hazing."

Professor Davis chuckled as Tony stared in disbelief at what he had just said.

"More like torture. Hazing is for people who join a fraternity or sorority or a club of some kind. This was torture."

"Are you sure, Tony?" The professor looked around the room and said, "Quiet everyone. Quiet please!"

"Tony and Ping, on behalf of the committee, I want to congratulate you both. Tony, I would like to present you with two things that I think you might enjoy. First, the manuscript."

Tony looked at what he was being handed. What he saw made the hair on the back of his neck stand up.

Relationships and Loops

Tony Simms, Sr.

"You are not the first Simms to discover loops. This was a paper your dad wrote to describe his ideas about getting things done in business. He prepared it as a handout when I invited him to speak to a class I was teaching. At the time, he said that the idea had come from conversations with other successful businesspeople in town. These individuals said that getting the right things done was critical to their success.

"As time went on, your dad began referring to this phenomenon as 'closing loops.' The loops you discovered were in a sense planted by your dad."

Professor Davis saw that Tony was having trouble keeping it together, and he paused for a moment, patted Tony on the back, and whispered, "Your dad would be so proud."

Tony did not attempt to hide his tears, and he stood proudly with a gentle smile on his face. *I think he would be proud.*

"Your dad fashioned small golden loops and, over the years, gave them to those who seemed to get things done. The group that emerged never met, but they all knew who they were. Somewhere along the way, they began referring to themselves as the 'Closed-Loop Society.' Everyone on this committee owns a golden loop. Everyone you met with has a golden loop."

Closed-Loop Society?

"A society whose members can be identified by their success in business and by what they carry in their pocket."

The good professor reached into his left pocket and pulled out a golden loop. "This golden loop was given to me by your father. I carry it with me as a reminder of how important it is to finish what I start, to marry dreams with action. I also keep it with me to remind me of the good times I had with my best friend."

He then reached into his right pocket and pulled out another golden loop. "And here is yours. This one belonged to your dad, as you can see by the inscription. There is no doubt in my mind that he would not only want you to have it but also would agree that you deserve it. You are now a member of the Closed-Loop Society. That and two dollars will get you a cup of coffee at the Lava Java." With this, they all laughed.

"None of us wanted to get too serious about ourselves or our *secret* society.

"This loop carries with it the responsibility that was once your dad's. It is now your job to identify and welcome new members into the group. There has not been a new member since your dad passed away.

"And in case you had anyone specific in mind when you first exercise this new responsibility, I have what you need."

Tony looked at the small box Professor Davis took off the table, a box wrapped in gold paper, and smiled. "Would it be something with the words *Ping Wang* inscribed on it?"

"Indeed it would." He handed the box to Tony.

Tony walked over to Ping, who was standing by his mother.

"Ping. Your work on the Student Loop Group has been critical, and you really know how to get things done. As my first official act as the conveyer of the loop, I want you to have this symbol of your membership in the Closed-Loop Society. Do you accept our invitation?"

"Indeed I do. Thank you."

Many hugs and handshakes later, and while the committee members talked and picked at a golden cake, Tony's mother took his arm. She took his golden loop in her hand and said, "Loop closed, Son."

Then she looked across the room at the vibrant Ping, who was in animated conversation, smiled, and whispered, "Loop open."

LANGUAGE OF LOOPS: A GLOSSARY

Closed loop A task that has been completed. A confirmation that information has been received. A loop that is closed in a timely fashion also may be known as *accountability* and/or the act of *execution*. It is a job done correctly and within the expected time frame.

Culture Vision moments are the building blocks of your culture. How well or poorly your vision moments are executed, each one being a loop closed, adds up to *become* your business's culture.

Experience zones The places in your business with the largest number of customer contacts and experiences that will make an impact on how your customer perceives you as a business. How well you manage these experience zones ultimately will affect your customer negatively or positively.

Innovation A strategic approach to growing your business and changing and improving your product. It is how you plan to look at creating, manufacturing, marketing, and delivering your product. Innovation is change. How you manage it will have short- and long-term effects on the success of your business.

In the loop A person who has been communicated with and is up to speed with the available facts or information.

Leadership Inspiring others to follow a course of action and following a belief in a mission or vision.

Leading by example This is the first step to true leadership. The leader lives the doctrine of the business. When the leader "goes first" in action. As Stephen Covey says, "When the leader walks his or her talk."

Loops in the process Tasks that are being worked on but are not done at this point. There is no such thing as a large loop. All loops are equal. Things that appear to be a large loop are actually a group of small interlinked loops.

Loop groups An *external* loop group is simply a group of peers who do not compete with each other and wish to share ideas, concepts, and thoughts regarding business. This could be a local group of different business leaders or even a group of the same business types from a nonlocal area. An *internal* loop group is a group of workers from within your company who come together to plan, solve problems, strategize, or simply discuss issues regarding your company.

Margins Leaving margins allows you to provide a cushion, or contingency, for the unknown or unexpected. Margins may be involved in the area of budgeting, time allocation, and in a more personal sense, even the level of a person's fitness. The more fit we are, the greater is the margin for becoming deconditioned or even ill.

Master loop closer (MLC) A person who has demonstrated, over a significant period of time, the ability to consistently and effectively close loops, thus significantly affecting his or her business, family, and community in a positive manner. A master loop closer may carry the designation of *MLC* after his or her name.

Open loop A task that has yet to be done. This could be a delegation, on a to-do list, or even a work assignment.

Out of the loop A person who has not been communicated with and is not up to speed on the facts or does not have the proper information.

Plan B An alternative plan that you may fall back on if in fact your initial plan, plan A, doesn't work out as expected. Plan B is usually best to have been created before it is needed, although in some instances it can be created in the flow of the process. This allows for greater flexibility as needed.

Standardized process A predefined system by which tasks or a group of tasks is completed. The object is for this system to be followed exactly the same each time according to predefined standardized procedures. This is accountability in action!

Vision moments The moment-to-moment actions of employees as they interface with your customers. These moments are a manifestation of the fundamental commitment to the vision of the company. This fundamental commitment guides each employee to accept responsibility for creating the vision at each opportunity. In a perfect world, they are actually acting out your corporate vision.

MODEL OF LOOPS:
THE LOOPOGRAM

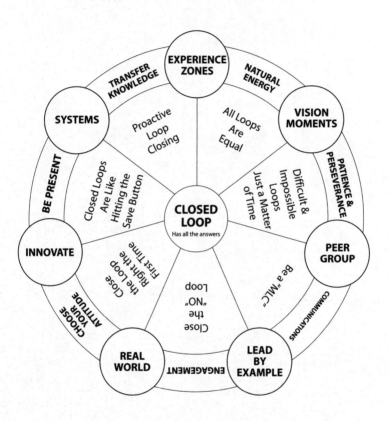

CLOSING LOOPS: MARY'S SEVEN LESSONS

Mary Chaet, MLC

I've always taken pride in my ability to close loops. I didn't notice that other people noticed until one day when my husband, Mike, was arranging for every single person in our office to read a very important book called *The War of Art*, by Steven Pressfield. After everyone had read the book and I still hadn't been asked to, I became a bit irritated and asked Mike, "Why?" He simply looked at me, smiled, and said, "Because you could have written this book!"

With that said, here are what I think are the seven most important lessons you can learn about closing loops.

1. Don't put off until tomorrow what you could have done yesterday.

The early bird gets the worm. Call it what you like. Closing loops creates efficiency. Efficiency increases productivity. The better you get at closing loops, the more productive you and your company will become. The sooner you close a loop, the sooner you can start on the next one. Furthermore, in many instances, closing a loop early on helps others to be more effective in their loop-closing journey.

2. All loops are created equal.

All loops are important. There is no such thing as an unimportant loop, and it's the closing of *all* the loops that marks the completion of a project.

Never look at a loop as being too big or too overwhelming to complete. Never look at a loop as being too small. An entire project may depend on that one "small" loop. Big loops are simply lots and lots of small loops all connected together.

3. Learn to close the "no" loop.

Focus on *your* loops. Learn to say "No." Do not try to close other people's loops. That is their job. Spend *your* time closing *your* loops. Working on just your loops will guarantee ample time to close them properly and close them well. Also learn to identify when you need to say "No" and give some loops to others to close.

4. Difficult loops take time. Impossible loops take a little more time. Impossible is simply an opinion.

Some loops can be closed in moments. Others take days, weeks, months, and even years. But there is no such thing as impossible. That's just someone else's opinion. Persevere until you get the "impossible" loop closed.

5. Closing loops is like hitting the SAVE button.

Probably one of the most important buttons on your computer is the SAVE button. What is more irritating than having spent an incredible amount of time on something, only to have forgotten to hit the SAVE button, and then, suddenly, all that you have been working on is gone! Closing loops is like hitting your SAVE button. If you learn how to close loops successfully, at the end of the day, you will feel great accomplishment at all you have done. The compilation of closing all those little loops adds up to a productive day. And with each small loop closed, you have put yourself in a closer position to closing some of those bigger loops on another day. A very important part of closing loops is *communicating* those closed loops to the appropriate people. This simple task generally speeds up the closing of loops in other departments.

6. Close your loops right the first time.

Prevention is a wonderful thing. Prevention of frustration. Prevention of unnecessary work or expensive redos. Prevention of wasted time, energy, and money. When you have a loop to close that is time-sensitive, generally the earlier you get it done, the better it is for everyone, especially you, the loop closer.

Example: You are holding a conference and need to line up the hotel for meeting/sleeping rooms. For some reason, this task gets overlooked, and when you finally get around to finalizing these details, all the hotels in your area are booked, and now, to complete your task, you either have to change your conference dates or you have to hold your events at two separate hotels in order to accommodate the number of people in your group. Having to use two hotels instead of one now opens up the possibility of all sorts of new problems for you to solve. Wouldn't it have been easier to confirm your hotel first thing and thus prevent all these potential problems?

7. Become a Master Loop Closer (MLC).

Not everyone is born an MLC, but that doesn't mean that you can't become one. Especially if you want to. When you learn to close loops, you'll find that you are working at a lower stress level. You'll find yourself with extra time. You'll find your job more enjoyable. And others will want to work with you because when you *say* what you'll do, you then *do* what you say. Become an MLC by mastering the other six loop-closing lessons.

MORE ABOUT LOOPS

Loops is more than a book, it is a management philosophy for small business. With that said, there is so much more information and opportunities that we would like to share with you.

Loops Workshops, Speakers, and Training

Loops workshops may be arranged in your area or even at your location.

For details simply log on to the Loops Web site www.loops4biz.com and click on Workshops and Training.

Become a Certified and Licensed Loops Coach

Start you own local Closed-Loop Society, or your own Small Business Loops Practice.

E-mail loopmaster@loops4biz.com for information.

Get on the Loops E-mail Lists for Regular Updates

Go to the Web site and register www.loops4biz.com

For Bulk Book Purchases

Contact the Loops4Biz office for quotes and instructions.

For More Loops Info

Or to contact Steve or Mike:

Web site: www.loops4biz.com

e-mail: loopmaster@loops4biz.com

call the LOOPS HOTLINE at 406-422-4656

Snail mail at:

LOOPS4BIZ

Box 1156

Helena, Montana 59624

ABOUT THE AUTHORS

Mike Chaet, Ph.D., has spent much of his professional time devloping and running small businesses. He is a small business marketing and management consultant, highly skilled in seminar communications. Since 1965 many of the businesses have been in the health club industry.

He was the winner of the 1983–1984 National Industry Service award, and in 1993 was named by *CBI* magazine as one of the fitness industry's 100 VIPs along with the likes of Jane Fonda and Arnold Schwarzenegger. In 1995, he was awarded the Lifetime Achievement Award by *Bodylife* magazine for his work in the European club industry. He was recently presented the Lifetime Achievement Award for his contributions to the Canadian fitness industry (Can Fit Pro).

Mike was founder and president of Club Marketing and Management Services, Inc. consulting firm, as well as M & M Property Management Company.

Chaet is a contributing author to many national magazines including *CBI*, *Club Industry*, and *Bodylife*, the German and French club trade publication. He has been a guest lecturer to such organizations as IHRSA, Club Industry, NYMCA, and Bodylife. Mike has been involved in the development of small businesses in more than 60 countries. He spent time as chief executive officer of a public corporation, as well as a 7-year stay with the prestigious Los Angeles Athletic Club. Along the way he has owned and operated his own clubs. As a consultant he has been involved in the development or management of over 2,500 different small businesses worldwide. He physically visits more than 1,000 small businesses per year and, having reached two million qualifying miles, was recently awarded Platinum Plus Medallion status from Delta Airlines, about which his wife Mary was not all that excited.

Mike and Mary live in Big Sky Country, Helena, Montana with their two pugs Ozzie and Mosie.

Contact Mike at loopmaster@loops4biz.com.

Stephen Lundin, Ph.D., is a writer, speaker, entrepreneur, and filmmaker with a rich history in business, management, and graduate level business education. He has written a number of books including the multimillion-copy bestselling *FISH!* and the simply bestselling *FISH! Tales, FISH! Sticks* and *FISH! for Life. Top Performer, A Bold Approach to Sales and Service* was published in January 2007 and has been adopted by a major hotel chain. *CATS: The Nine Levels of Innovation*, published in January of 2009, was quickly adopted by a medical products company. *Ubuntu*, a book written to upgrade the contemporary workplace by drawing on powerful African values, will be published by Random House in the spring of 2010.

During the last decade Steve has worked with hundreds of companies around the globe. The government of Abu Dhabi; the largest builder in Dubai; nursing homes in New Zealand; banking systems in Africa, Australia, and Malaysia; a shipping company in Singapore; the Japanese, Singapore, and Australian Management Institutes; and health club chains in Sweden and Portugal are a few of his international clients. U.S. clients include a cross section of the Fortune 500 and a variety of nonprofit and government entities. The experiences gained in working with this diverse set of clients affords him a broad platform from which to view leadership, innovation, quality of work life, customer service, and change.

Contact Steve at slrunner@aol.com.